Karen Sheridan offers a vital tool for every woman who wants to be self-sufficient and proactive while taking charge of her money life. The Money Mystique *isn't just about money—it's about you. Not only is this a practical and useful tool, it's downright fun to read. A book like this doesn't come along very often.*

—Olivia Mellan, psychotherapist and
author of *Money Harmony* and
Overcoming Overspending

THE **MONEY MYSTIQUE**

A WOMAN'S GUIDE TO ACHIEVING LIFETIME FINANCIAL CONFIDENCE

KAREN SHERIDAN

NEW HARBINGER PUBLICATIONS, INC.

Publisher's Note

This book is intended to provide guidance in regard to money management and life issues in general. It is understood that the author and the publisher are not herein offering investment advice. It is further understood that they are not rendering any professional services, including legal, accounting, or tax advice. If such services and advice are required, professional assistance should be sought.

The stories included in the text are representations and not actual life stories. The facts have been altered to protect the identity of any individual(s).

The Money Mystique® is a trademark owned by Karen Sheridan.
Distributed in the U.S.A. by Publishers Group West; in Canada by Raincoast Books; in Great Britain by Airlift Book Company, Ltd.; in South Africa by Real Books, Ltd.; in Australia by Boobook; and in New Zealand by Tandem Press.

Copyright © 2000 by Karen Sheridan
New Harbinger Publications, Inc.
5674 Shattuck Avenue
Oakland, CA 94609

Cover design by Poulson/Gluck Designs
Text design by Michele Waters

Library of Congress Catalog Card Number: 00-134869
ISBN 1-57224-222-1 Paperback

New Harbinger Publications' Web site address: www.newharbinger.com

02   01   00

10   9   8   7   6   5   4   3   2   1

First printing

Dedication

I dedicate this book to you wonderful women who have honored me with your life stories. I am touched by your courage and commitment. And I am filled with gratitude for your willingness to open your hearts, your minds, and your eyes to the possibilities life holds for you. Thank you from the bottom of my heart for your enthusiasms and support. You have enriched my life beyond measure.

CONTENTS

INTRODUCTION

"Riches come from management rather than from revenue."

Michel de Montaigne (1533–1592)

This book is for every woman who wants to learn how to use money to create a life worth living. A life she loves. A life that expresses and reflects who she is, who she has determined herself to be. Money is an essential element for creating such a life. It is a necessary tool.

I love to help women understand how to use money to create exciting and fulfilling lives. To that end, I spend most of my time talking with women about money. Sometimes we meet privately, other times we meet in large, public venues, such as conventions and workshops. But my message is always the same: To create the life that you want for yourself, you must learn how to manage your money wisely.

Our society proclaims and perpetuates the idea that women don't manage money very well. Popular folklore holds that we know how to *spend* money—not how to earn it, keep it, or grow it. But this is not true! Millions of women use money wisely, whether small sums or large. Every woman can do this. You can, too. It is true, though, that many women report feeling inadequate to the challenge of managing their money. Many feel afraid. Some even feel lost. The sense of well-being that comes from managing money effectively eludes them. It is as if there were a secret mystique to managing money. But there is no such secret. Once you learn the language of money and know how money works, everything falls into place.

Women and Dependency

I think one reason so many women feel lost is that they abdicate responsibility for managing their money to someone else, be it husband, father, brother, or stockbroker. This is the easy way out. But it also serves to reinforce the idea that someone else—usually and preferably male—is better at taking care of a woman's finances than she is herself.

When a life-changing event such as divorce or widowhood comes along, however, many dependent women discover just how vulnerable they really are. Often, they have spent their lives taking care of everyone else in their families, but no one has taken care of them. Moreover, they haven't taken very good care of themselves. They have not paid much attention to what *they* want and need.

As they age, such women become sadly disillusioned. They suddenly discover that their money is gone and they are poor. The retirement money isn't what they assumed it would be, and nobody can fix that. There is no one there to fix it. They struggle to pay their bills when they thought they'd be enjoying carefree "golden years." I've met women who eat popcorn for dinner so they can afford to buy a birthday gift for their grandchild.

The Facts

There are numerous statistics that reinforce the idea that women need to pay more attention to money throughout their lives. Consider the following information.

1. Poverty is a much more common experience for women than for men. Throughout their adult years, women have a 50 percent greater risk of being poorer than men. During old age, the risk is 70 percent greater (U.S. Congress 1992).

2. Almost three-quarters of elderly persons living below the poverty level are women (U.S. Dept. of Labor 1992).

3. Almost four times as many widows live in poverty than do wives of the same age. More than half of the widows who are poor were not poor before their husbands died (U.S. Dept. of Labor 1992).

4. Seven out of ten women born between 1946 and 1964 will outlive their husbands. Many can expect to be widows for fifteen to twenty years (U.S. Dept. of Labor 1992).

5. Women average 11.5 years away from the labor force, while men average 1.3 years (U.S. Congress 1992). Yet more than half of all adult Americans say it is likely they will be responsible for the care of an elderly parent or relative in the next ten years. And 72 percent of caregivers are women (U.S. Dept. of Labor 1992).

6. Women have achieved educational parity with men. Yet women continue to be overrepresented in administrative support and service occupations. The median earnings of women age twenty-five years and over, who worked full-time, earned 73 percent of their male counterpart's earnings in 1998. (U.S. Dept. of Commerce 2000).

Cultural Influences

When women know how to use money, we become confident and strong. When we know we are making financial choices based on facts, not fantasies, we become comfortable, easy, and gracious in our financial dealings. We make sensible choices that support us throughout our lives and we don't have to live without the things we want. Our fears about money don't control us.

The Necessity for Self-Awareness

Self-awareness is the critical first step of managing your money properly. If you don't understand yourself and what you want in your life, all the money in the world won't make you feel secure or content. For example, you need to know how you feel about money and the meaning you place on money in your life. You need to have a clear idea of what you want to bring into your life and how to think differently so that money is not an obstacle to your self-expression. You also need to understand the choices you have and how to make choices that support your goals. The more insight you have into yourself, the more clarity you will have about managing your money. Otherwise, how can you make sensible choices? You don't have to have everything figured out. But you do have to *start* figuring it out.

Throughout the book you will be asked questions. While you are reading, keep a separate journal to record your answers. Take time to write down your answers in your journal. When you write, you are forced to focus more deeply than if you merely read and think about the material. Do all of the chapter exercises in your journal. Review your answers frequently. Note that as you read, your answers may change.

 Think About It . . .

Begin your journal by answering these three basic questions:

1. *What do you want to gain from reading this book?*

2. *How do you relate to money?*

3. *Does the way you relate to money support the life you want?*

Write as much or as little as you choose. There are no right answers. Just write whatever is true for you.

Money and Security

You may think that having more money would solve all of your money problems. You may think a big bank account equals security. But this is not so. Security comes from believing in yourself. You are secure when you realize you are responsible for yourself, and you know you are up to the task. When you have the courage to listen to your own heart and you know how to take care of yourself, and you are willing to do so, you have the kind of strength that no one can take from you. Peace of mind comes from knowing that, given your particular circumstances, you are making the best decisions possible. Once you make this internal shift, there is no turning back. The path of self-responsibility may be frightening at times, but the rewards are beyond measure.

Managing Your Money

When women take on the job of managing their money, we quickly figure out that the key word is "managing." Except in cases of extreme poverty, what you do with your money is more important than the amount you have to work with. If you mismanage $20,000 a year, it is very likely that you will mismanage $40,000 a year.

Managing money is an art, not a science. Even though you are working with numbers, there is never only one right answer. When women really think about what we want out of life—that is, when we know what our core values are—and what we want from our money—we learn to use it wisely. We may still become emotional about money, but we don't make financial decisions or direct our lives based solely on those emotions. We are able to set boundaries around our feelings and integrate reason into the total picture. We don't allow our emotions to rule us.

Money Is a Metaphor

The way women treat money can be seen as a metaphor for the way we treat ourselves. When we treat money as if it is not important, we feel we are not important. Women who are fearful about money feel they don't matter very much.

A woman who understands how to manage money in a manner consistent with her life goals respects herself and respects her money. She knows where her money is. She doesn't stuff twenty dollar bills carelessly into her handbag or leave them stashed for months in a coat pocket buried in the back of a closet. She doesn't misfile stock certificates or lose checkbooks. She treats her money with the same kind of respect that she treats herself and anything of value. She doesn't need to worry or obsess about her money, because she knows how much she has to work with, and where it is.

When a woman has an unhealthy relationship with money, it often surfaces as a continuing chaotic drama. How to pay for this emergency or that temptation? *What's my account balance? How could I possibly be overdrawn, again?* I think some of us get caught up in these familiar dramas because they keep us from facing our deeper, real-life issues. They keep us stuck and struggling, small, and dependent.

I encourage you to give up on the drama and chaos, and face your money issues squarely. When you have the courage to learn about managing your money properly, your barriers to success evaporate. As you tone down your dramas about money, you become able to see clearly and choose wisely. Your attention shifts from the limitations of the current moment to the big picture of what you want and how you can manifest it. You begin creating rather than merely reacting.

I envision a world where women are willing and able to take care of ourselves. This doesn't mean that we have to earn a wage. It doesn't mean that we have to leave our families. It doesn't mean we have to stop caring about others. It does mean that we have to make choices that support us—choices consistent with our needs and values.

When women take responsibility for managing our personal finances, we become better partners, better parents, better adult children, and better workers. Taking personal responsibility assumes a willingness to act rather than react; to be strong rather than weak; to speak up rather than remain silent. The world needs women who are willing to make difficult choices and stand firm. It needs women willing to demonstrate to their children that they are taking good care of themselves. Society needs women to change how they show up in the world. Change happens one step at a time, one woman at a time.

Showing up in the world as a confident, competent woman is the greatest gift a woman can give to her children. She can teach them that "feminine" and "competent" are not contradictions. Children learn from observation. When they have a mother (and father) who is competent with money, they are very likely to become competent adults themselves. Conflict about money may be the biggest cause of divorce in America. When all parties feel free to express their feelings and ideas about money, family relationships are strengthened.

Strength, Weakness, and Money

When women fully embrace their power, they unconsciously influence others to do the same. I encourage you to pay attention, to understand your power, to hold on to it, and to use it for good in the world. A strong woman teaches her boss and coworkers that she is competent and capable. She knows what she wants and asks for it. She is proud of her skills and experience, and she wants to be compensated properly. She can be soft, too, because she knows that softness and strength go together, hand in glove.

A strong woman does not need to be strident. Such a woman knows the difference between assertiveness and aggressiveness. When a woman feels strong, she also feels free—and she encourages others to be free as well. Sadly, I have met many women who don't feel strong. They do not honor themselves or the world. They discourage themselves and others. They hang on to resentments. They hide behind their fears and are quick to list the many injustices the world has set upon them. Life happens to them. They feel stuck. They feel like victims.

Nevertheless, I believe these women are really strong women in hiding. I believe any woman, given the choice, would choose strength. And (here's the secret clue) I believe we give strength to ourselves. We get to choose who we are and how we live. We get to choose whether we live from our strength or our weakness. No one else and nothing outside of us will give us permission to move from weakness to strength.

Weak women become strong women when they choose to change their minds, their attitudes, and their habits. When they choose to examine their lives and enact the desired changes, they change. One sure sign of weakness turning into strength occurs when women start dealing with the money issues in their lives.

My work makes me hopeful for the future. I have witnessed stunning transformations among women who are changing the world by changing themselves. They aren't afraid to talk about money. They make choices consistent with who they are. They are grounded in reality and accept themselves as they are. They don't buy into popular consumer culture. They listen to their hearts and act from quiet strength.

Living from the Inside Out

This book was written for women who want to learn how to use money to enhance their lives. Knowing how to create and use money certainly contributes to a sense of well-being. Grace and comfort with money create grace and comfort in life. If a woman truly wants to be free, she has to face her fears. The only way out is to go inward—to yourself. Know yourself. Manage yourself. I like the way Barbara Stanny, the author of *Prince Charming Isn't Coming: How Women Get Smart About Money* (1997) puts it: "If you don't deal with your money, your money will deal with you."

This book is intended to help you shift and change your feelings about money so that you will begin to use it in a healthy way. If you thoughtfully work through the process, you will have a better sense of yourself. You will know how to use money to expand, not limit yourself. The final hurdle women face in our pursuit of social equality lies in our unwillingness to manage money. We will continue to be second-class citizens until we have the courage to pay attention to money as if it mattered—as if we mattered. Equality cannot be bestowed upon us. It must be earned.

How to Use This Book

There isn't any right way to read this book. Review the chapter headings and dive in anywhere. You don't need to read every word and every chapter. Find the passages that speak to you right now. Use a highlighter and mark the book up. Write in the margins. Write in your journal. Do the exercises. You learn better when you are active. Engage!

The exercises are important. Keep it simple. All you need is a journal to write down your thoughts and feelings and answer the questions. They will help you solve the mystery of managing the money in your life once and for all. The last chapters are designed to give you a model for writing a financial plan and putting it into action. These will be the final steps on your path to financial freedom. This is the place for you to work with your real-life circumstances. And you only need a pencil and paper.

Read with your own life experiences in mind. Take the concepts seriously, but not too seriously. Read with a quiet mind. Understand that the journey to self-understanding takes time. As you progress, you will observe subtle changes in your attitudes about and understanding of money. You may feel a bit anxious at times. Trust that the rewards will be well worth it. One day you will be amazed to discover that you can't remember the last time you worried about money.

Observe how your body feels as you read. If you feel a fullness in your throat or a pain in your stomach, try to determine where it comes from. You may feel angry. Or sad. You may even laugh, seeing yourself in another woman's story. I hope you feel something, because that will mean you are opening up to incredible possibilities. Pass this book along to your friends and family. Share it with anyone who will listen. Talk about money. Your silence keeps you stuck.

Find people who exercise their own power and honor you for doing the same. Converse with other women. Share your stories. Tell the truth—about yourself and about money. Notice yourself shifting, growing, expanding. Pay attention to your feelings, moods, and cycles. Notice what you believe is possible for your life. Observe yourself and celebrate yourself! Continue educating yourself about money. Learning is a never-ending process. Read other books. Listen to financial stories in the news. Read the business and finance sections of the newspaper. You learn just by paying attention.

Live, love, and work from the core belief that you are creating the life you want by making conscious money choices, every day. Remember—you are important. Don't give up. Don't fall asleep. Don't let someone else handle your life. You are the very best person to handle your own life and your own money. Step up to the plate. You can do it!

CHAPTER ONE

HOW DID WE GET HERE?

Today, when I read about powerful women in business and government, I marvel to think how far we've come. It is commonplace to see women pursuing economic roles traditionally reserved for men. This is true in all sectors of the economy. It is also true that many women are more eager to earn money than they are to manage it after they get it. They are either too busy or just not interested. This is a tragic mistake. Ignoring the link between earning money and managing it puts women at risk of financial disaster as they age.

The Women's Movement

Taking a look at where we've been helps us to understand where we are. So I would like to take a brief look back at the women's movement of the late 1960s and early 1970s because I think it will help you to understand our world of today. The impact of raising women's awareness and status has changed our world dramatically. I will also provide some personal history because my success, like many other women's achievements, was a part of the women's movement.

As a girl growing up in the 1950s, I believed that a woman's role was to take care of the household while her husband worked. I was programmed to grow up, get married, have children, and be happy. And I did exactly that. I married in the early 1960s and promptly produced two children. My husband earned the money and I spent it. He took very good care of us. I loved being a mother. Life was easy. I was happy at home and I never gave voice to the part of myself that longed to break free. I had read *The Feminine Mystique* by Betty Friedan. I was content to stay home with my children in 1963, but after a while I experienced a subtle shift deep inside.

I knew there was more to life. But I didn't want to rock the boat. When my children started high school, I saw that I would soon be out of a job at home. The time had come to add another dimension to my life. I joined the army of working women and marched into the workforce. I was excited and I was scared.

By 1975, the women's movement was in full bloom. The women in the movement were angry—at society's institutions, at business, and at men. We believed that if we could get jobs, we would achieve economic security and power and be able to live richer, more independent lives. We were tired of second-class citizenship. We wanted the same opportunities in the workplace that our husbands and fathers had. We thought we were missing out on something grand—the opportunity to make money. We believed we deserved equality and were determined to have it. And we didn't want to wait. It was an exciting time to be a woman. We were ready to take on the world. We marched on private men's clubs and on Washington. We marched out of the house and into the marketplace.

The Old Economy and Women

History shows that social changes usually have economic roots. The women's movement is no exception. By 1974, the U.S. economy had changed dramatically from the postwar boom of the 1950s and 1960s. The stock market stalled in 1973, and with the onset of the oil crisis in 1974 inflation started to spiral out of control. The miraculous increases in the standard of living that Americans had enjoyed since the end of World War II, sputtered, rolled over, and died.

I remember hearing a guest on *The Phil Donahue* Show in the '70s proclaim that my generation, which had grown up in the 1950s, was the last generation that would enjoy a higher standard of living than their parents. I couldn't believe my ears. The idea was unthinkable. There I was raising my two children in a big house in an affluent suburb. We had two cars in the garage, a microwave oven, and instant hot water. We were living much better than our parents and we didn't even question it. But inflation changed our reality. Our economic bubble burst while we waited in the gas line. The world had changed. We had no idea by how much. By the time my children were grown, stay-at-home moms had become the exception. It wasn't easy for one person to make enough money to provide for a family.

The women's movement and the changed economy seemed made for each other. It was perfect somehow. Not only did women want to go to work, they had to go to work. By 1997, 59.8 percent of women over the age of sixteen were in the labor force or looking for work. Only 13 percent of married families fit the traditional model of husband as wage earner and wife as homemaker. Today, in 61 percent of married-couple families, both husband and wife work outside the home (U.S. Census Bureau 1999a).

The 1980s also accelerated the consumer culture. Television became a prime motivator to consume. We entered the age of "He who dies with the most toys wins." By 1990 it took two full-time salaries to support the cars, houses, and electronics the standard middle-class American household wanted. We learned some hard lessons about the difficulties of combining a career with family. Today millions of women, even those with big jobs and million-dollar incomes, know how difficult it is to leave their children with someone else all day and return home too tired to enjoy their families.

The New Economy and Women

Today, we are in the throes of another economic and social revolution. Currently, the U.S. enjoys the most exciting economic expansion in history. Once again, it has become possible for one person to support a family. The standard of living began to improve in 1997. For the first time in twenty-four years, the real income of American families grew. This means that many young families are once again separating the household duties. The women are taking time out from work to care for the children while the men are providing the economic support. I have recently noticed many young wives and mothers whose husbands earn enough money to support a family. These women are choosing not to go to work but to stay home and raise their children. These families have learned that it's marvelous for one parent to be home with the children. Usually that parent is the mother. This is good for families, but it places these women in a precarious position financially.

Women at Risk

With all the progress women have made in recent decades one might think the model of how men and women relate to each other had changed. But in my experience it hasn't. It seems to me that both men and women still believe a man is more capable of managing money than a woman. In most marriages or partnerships it is still true that the person who makes the money, or the most money, has the most power. And because women often earn less than men that person is usually the man.

Even though the opportunities are there, many women don't pay as much attention to their work life as they do to their personal life. We move in and out of the job market, so we don't build up retirement benefits. Contributions to retirement plans are based on salary. Women don't make as much as men, so we don't have the opportunity to put as much money away.

We also enter the workforce later in life, after our children are raised, so we can't put in the time it takes for retirement money to grow. Many women who are barely making ends meet laugh at the suggestion that they should put money away for their future. They need it right now. But if they don't put the money away and they are barely squeaking by at thirty-five, where will they be at seventy-five?

How I Learned to Manage Money

In 1980, my children were in high school and I was ready to make the break from the suburbs to downtown. It took me three months to find a job managing a securities law firm. It was quite a challenge to integrate the demands of a new job with my chores at home. I did my best, but my husband walked out the door within a year

By 1981, I was divorced with two children. As I look back on it, I find it curious that I didn't expect my husband to take care of me financially after I was no longer taking care of him at home. Even though I had been at home for most of our marriage, I didn't ask for much in the way of support. I preferred to split our assets down the middle and go our separate ways. I believed that I should take financial responsibility for myself from that moment forward. I didn't feel afraid. I was exhilarated to be taking care of myself for the first time in my life.

I was lucky. For some unknown reason, I have always believed that I could take care of myself. I don't know where that belief came from. Certainly, most women of my generation were raised to believe that the husband makes money, the wife doesn't. Somehow I didn't internalize that message. I saw people making money in the stock market, so I decided to invest. I didn't know a stock from a mutual fund, but I knew I could learn. For the first few years, I lost money on every investment I made. I didn't even know what I didn't know.

I realized I needed to learn how to invest or I wasn't going to be very successful.

I learned that the stock market is about business and that business is about people, what they buy, what they sell, and the choices they make. It is the human element in business and the stock market that still fascinates me, even after all these years. I have a healthy respect for entrepreneurs and managers of businesses, both large and small. These people often risk everything to start a business and they succeed or fail according to market conditions, timing, and a willingness to see the future and change strategies in response to an ever-changing world. I learned that I can understand the economy, the impact it has on companies, and on people like you and me. And I learned that I can learn, even though I am not good at math and I had no business background. I was a sponge during those first years. I wanted to know everything.

After six years of working and learning, I landed a job as vice president of a large international money management firm on Wall Street. This was the center of the action. By that time, I knew enough so that I was able to help other people manage their money. Working on Wall Street gave me an education money can't buy. I had never thought about money as a source of happiness. It was true I had more fun when I had more money, but having a lot of money didn't seem like a life or death issue to me. However, talking to wealthy people about their portfolios changed my views about the role money plays in a person's life.

Most of my clients were women of wealth. They lived in Park Avenue apartments with all the accoutrements. They owned original artwork, fur coats, expensive china, and serious jewelry—the works. To my way of thinking, they should have felt financially comfortable with all of their possessions and a few million dollars. But time and again I noticed they were not comfortable. They lived in fear. I couldn't understand it until I realized they didn't know very much about managing their money. And they knew they didn't know.

Most of these women had inherited their money and didn't have a good sense of where it came from. They lived in fear that somebody would take advantage of them. (They probably were easy prey for unscrupulous con artists.) They were afraid to open their eyes and take responsibility for their money. And they were afraid to stay in the dark.

At first, their ideas and feelings confused me. We would talk about money, but the underlying conversation had very little to do with money. My clients were aware they needed money to maintain their lifestyle—and they had enough money. Yet they were afraid. I didn't understand it until I realized they didn't know how to be responsible for their money—and themselves. I realized they were fearful because they didn't know how to manage their money. This realization changed my life. I decided that I wanted to teach other women how to manage their money so they wouldn't have to live in fear.

I will never forget meeting one wonderful woman who was in her late seventies. She "guessed" her portfolio was worth about $8 million. She had never looked at it or talked about it with anyone. She wasn't comfortable discussing money, and she had no idea of what she owned. After months of coaxing, she agreed to meet me and an associate at our office and to bring all of her financial information with her.

She arrived at the appointed time, carrying two large brown shopping bags. When she turned the bags upside down and dumped out the papers, stock certificates, and bearer bonds, I couldn't believe my eyes. Her entire financial past and future were stuffed into a couple of shopping bags. It took us two days to sort through the piles.

We separated the stocks from the bonds. We tossed out the ten-year-old junk mail. She owned bonds that had matured more than twenty years ago. If the company was still in business, she could get her principal back. But she had missed out on thousands of dollars in interest. We found stock certificates for companies that were no longer in existence as the same entity. They had merged, been acquired, or gone out of business. She was delighted when we discovered her late husband's Last Will and Testament. She said she had "always wondered where that darn thing went."

When all was said and done, her portfolio was worth about $3 million. Certainly she had enough money to last her the rest of her life. But her *opportunity cost* was enormous. That means she had forfeited the substantial return she could have made on her money if it had been invested.

She had no heirs. But had she been willing to take responsibility for her investments earlier in her life, she could have done so much more with her money. She could have donated to her favorite charities, or championed causes, people, and projects. She could have done so many more good works in the world. But her reluctance to talk about her money had stopped her.

Because of her fears about money her financial loss was small compared to the small life she was living. She worried about money every single day. However, this story ends happily. Eventually, she talked with us about her goals and how she could manage her money to meet her needs. She became quite confident with her spending and investing. She doesn't worry anymore because she knows what she has and how much she can spend.

Women as Caretakers

Many women harbor a strong need to take care of others. We believe our true value lies in taking care of the people we love. We quit our jobs to take care of our children and sick parents. We may also want to express ourselves in our work rather than to make money. We may value being recognized for doing a good job and supporting others as a substitute for making money. We may find it difficult to talk about our salaries and benefits as if we deserved to be well-paid. As one client told me, "I might as well just say, 'That's okay, I'll work like a dog. You don't have to pay me much.'"

It feels good to be needed. It feels good to do good work. It also feels good to be taken care of. But, if such care comes at the expense of a woman taking herself seriously, it weakens her spirit. She has turned her power over to someone else. She may have to flatter and please someone else just to have enough food to eat and shelter for her children.

Many women fear becoming bag ladies. I hear this particular fear repeated over and over again. I hear it from some well-educated and successful women. Such fear often surprises me. These women nurture a core belief that they will outlive their money.

The truth is that many women are very vulnerable. Those who stay home and care for children while their husbands or partners bring in the money are at risk. Women in the marketplace who value giving service over getting paid are at risk. Those who live on trust funds or money other people made are at risk. Those who spend everything they make and don't put anything away for the future are at risk. Women who don't think money is important are at risk. Women who are afraid to handle money are at risk. It's as if they don't live in the reality of dealing with money and making life choices.

Older Women and Silent Poverty

Women are at the greatest risk of being poor when they are old. Often they don't wake up to this fact until they reach their mid-fifties. It is far more challenging to remedy the situation at that age than it is for younger women. Older women find it difficult to thrive in our youth-oriented culture. Older women who are poor find it nearly impossible. They become invisible. They have no voice. Poor women often feel shame, and try to hide their poverty from friends and family. They live with quiet desperation.

A widow in her mid-seventies told me she had been plunged into poverty the day her husband died. His pension payments had consisted of an annuity only on *his* life. She said they had not been able to afford to take joint life annuity payments on both of their lives because the payment was smaller. They had needed all the money they could get. Sadly, the payments stopped when her husband died. She receives nothing from the annuity, and is living on a few hundred dollars a month from his Social Security.

More Money Isn't Necessarily the Answer—Managing It Is

I've learned that the ability to genreate money has very little to do with the ability to manage it. My favorite example is my friend, Helen, who has been very successful at managing her money. When Helen was fifty, she retired with a million dollars in assets. She never married and she never inherited any money. She invested about ten percent of everything she ever earned. She bought stock in good companies with good reputations and good markets. She listened when people talked about investing. She lived very simply and took a few chances.

Helen understands how the stock market works. She is an unemotional investor. She doesn't worry when the value of her investments falls. Her money gives her freedom to live the life she chooses. She is able to help her friends and give money to women's shelters and various charitable organizations. She gets satisfaction from helping others. But not at her own expense.

Helen's story wouldn't be very interesting if it weren't for the following fact. She never had a huge income. Even though she worked hard, her highest gross income was $24,000 a year. Every time someone tells me they don't have enough money to invest, I think of Helen. Many people who say they don't have enough money to invest have incomes many times larger than Helen's. The difference between Helen and those people is that Helen was willing to live on less than she made. She was also willing to invest her money over a long period of time.

Her story illustrates a very important point. *The amount of money you have isn't as important as what you do with it.* It is possible for most working people to create wealth if they are willing to work and invest at the same time. Helen told me it took her twenty-five years to make her first million, three years to make her second, and one year to make her third.

 Think About It . . .

Now, in your journal write down your personal history regarding money. Think about your childhood and the lessons you learned about money. Make a list of your parents, other family members, teachers, and caregivers. Then describe their styles regarding money. Were they spendthrifts or big spenders? Did they have an emotional relationship with money? Next, think about your personal relationship to money as an adult. Write ten words that describe your relationship to money. Do any of these words surprise you? How well do you manage your money? What can you do to manage your money better?

Don't Assume Your Husband Is Planning for Your Retirement

Many women believe their husbands are taking care of the family's investments for the future. They are often surprised when this is not the case. They learn the money was spent on tuition for the kids, vacations, and big houses. They never questioned where the money came from or where it went. They participated in the illusion of financial well-being for as long as thirty or forty years.

This illusion works until the husband stops earning a paycheck. The minute he loses his job or retires, they are jolted into reality. The money to support the lifestyle just isn't there anymore. The mortgage payments haven't gone away, just the means to pay them. When these wives face this reality they become angry and scared. Many of them have never worked and they don't know what to do. Their husbands are tired and ready to retire. Many of these men have done their best and often feel they have very little to show for all their years in the workplace.

Here is an example: A couple in their sixties came to see me at the wife's insistence. They had lived a prosperous life for forty years.

They had been marvelous parents who wanted only the best for their children. They had often enjoyed family vacations in wonderful places. Their four children had attended the best schools. The husband, who is over sixty, recently lost his second job in the past five years due to the downsizing of the companies for which he worked. They had spent their savings while he was between jobs. Recently they ran out of money. Nothing had been invested for retirement. He has a small inheritance that will see them through for the next few years. When it is gone, they don't know what they will do.

The wife is frightened and furious. She had always assumed he was putting money away for retirement. She cannot believe she is in this precarious financial situation at her age. The bad news came as a total surprise because she had never asked a single question about their finances. He is angry too. He asks her, "How could I put money away when you were spending it as fast as I could make it?" They both feel like victims.

Today, thousands of women are making big money. But I wonder how many of them manage it competently. I observe a very low correlation between income (current earnings) and net worth (current assets). These women don't understand the need to invest a portion of their incomes for their future. They spend all of their money so they never build a significant net worth. This may seem astonishing, but it's true.

We Fear What We Don't Understand

I believe the best way to move from fear to enlightenment is through education. This is true for any subject. If you learn how to drive, you no longer fear driving. If you learn how to ski, you no longer fear skiing. If you learn how to manage money, you no longer fear money. Knowledge allows you to manage your fears so you can move ahead confidently. You may feel scared from time to time as you come across something you don't understand, but knowledge allows you to keep going even when you make a mistake or don't know exactly what to do.

Hundreds of women have told me they aren't "really interested" in money. It's "boring." Others tell me they "don't have time" to worry about money. Yet these women do worry about money. Some worry about it every single day. For many, the subject is too frightening to explore. It is easier to pretend it doesn't matter. It does matter, though, and ignoring it creates tremendous anxiety.

Those women who make commitments to take care of their money describe strong feelings of euphoria and being in control. They exchange worry for peace of mind. Managing money, like any other subject, takes time to understand and learn the nuances, but once you get it, you get it for life. You only have to learn once because once you know, you know.

The language of money is a foreign language. It can be intimidating. Money management practices aren't taught in school. Money isn't talked about in polite company. Anytime you encounter a language you don't understand, you feel out of place in the conversation. But you can learn the language of money, just as you can learn a foreign language. No one was born speaking Finance. Nobody came out of the womb asking, "What happened in the stock market today?" Everyone who knows the language of money had to learn it. It's not difficult. It just takes a commitment.

Learning how to manage your money may seem very easy to put off until another day. I know you are busy. I know there is too much to do and too little time. But some women spend more time trying to save ten cents on a gallon of gas than they do planning for their old age. Women spend considerably more time planning their weddings than they do planning their futures. Yet, only 43 percent of women over the age of sixty-five are married, and the median income of American women over age sixty-five was $10,504 in 1998 (U.S. Department of Commerce 1998). This makes a good case for managing your money as if your future depended on it. Because it does.

Making Friends with Money

Money is not a four-letter word. There is a money component in every decision we make. We make better decisions when we understand the money choices we have. I encourage women to talk about money—not occasionally, but all the time.

Honest dialogue about money helps you understand what you want and how you are going to get what you want. When you discuss your challenges with credit card debt or a bankruptcy, you find solace just in the telling. You also can teach your children that money isn't a taboo subject. It is just another topic. When you find the courage to share your money stories, you feel empowered and strong.

The financial opportunities available for women today were only a dream for my generation. I look forward to the day when women take full advantage of these opportunities. Women spend untold resources in the pursuit of money and few or no resources in learning how to manage it. This must change and that change can only come from within. This can't be legislated. The Money Revolution for women is an inside job. It doesn't matter whether you live with a man, another woman, your children, or alone. It's up to you and you alone to figure it out for yourself.

Your choice to read this book is important because it says you want to learn more about money and how to use it. As you read, try to fit my words and the stories of other women into the context of your own life. Challenge yourself. Challenge your friends. You will be amazed at how much fun it is to talk truthfully about money without the emotional overlay.

As you read, you will learn many things that will ease your anxiety. For example, you will learn that you don't have to be good at math to manage money. You've already learned that you don't have to have lots of money to manage it wisely. You will learn that you don't have to know everything. In fact, managing money is like learning to dance. Once you know the basics, you can be very creative. But you have to know the basics.

You will learn that it is all right to make mistakes. That's how you learn. Just don't beat yourself up. Move on and learn from your mistakes, don't mourn them. They are your best teachers. This is the education that will make the difference. I am still learning after more than twenty years. It is a lifelong process. You will learn that you can start right where you are. In fact, it is impossible to start anyplace else. Many women believe they need lots of money before they can invest. This is absolutely not true. You can create wealth by putting a small amount of money away over a long period of time. The amount of money that is invested isn't as important as the habit of investing. It is much simpler than it seems.

As you read the book, I suggest that you:

1. Keep an open mind. Be willing to question many of your assumptions about money. They may not serve you anymore.

2. Think about what you want to learn from this book. Think about what you already know about money and how you handle your money. What don't you know? Write some of your ideas in your journal before you start.

3 Examine where you are right now in your life. Look at the choices you have made that created your results. But go easy on yourself—look at your life without judgment.

4. Realize that you are absolutely unique. No two people have the same ideas or desires. What works for another person

may not work for you. What works for you may not work for anyone else. There is no one right answer for everybody.

5. Determine your own definition of wealth. I don't have a clue what wealth means. I often ask people to define wealth. The answer varies, usually according to the net worth of the person answering the question. Some people feel wealthy when they have ten dollars left over at the end of the month. Others with a wallet full of hundred-dollar bills feel poor. Some feel wealthy only in comparison to others. They think anyone who has more money than they do is wealthy. Your definition of wealth and your willingness to be "wealthy" creates your reality.

6. Finally, have fun. You have the rest of your life before you.

CHAPTER TWO

LISTENING TO THE STORIES YOU TELL YOURSELF ABOUT MONEY

Man prefers to believe that which he prefers to be true.

Francis Bacon (1561–1626)

Everything that you typically associate with money management—the planning and number crunching, the research, the intense consideration of various strategies and options—all come *after* you take the single most important step, which is understanding yourself and your emotions regarding money.

Creating Reality

We create our personal realities with our thoughts. Every day we have experiences that we interpret through our own unique lenses of perception. Your lens is not the same as anyone else's. You absorb experiences and information, you make the connections and figure things out. You create your own meaning. This meaning creates your reality. It becomes the story you tell to yourself, and to the world.

We spend our lives creating our realities every day. It happens when we aren't paying attention. We just go about our lives agreeing with our own versions of reality. New information comes in and is merged into agreement with the past. Our new experiences reinforce our old beliefs, and we feel secure that life is just the way it is, whether we like it or not.

Stories We Tell Ourselves

Storytelling is a wonderful art form and women are good storytellers. It's how we learn, connect, and pass along our wisdom. I've noticed that women are especially good at telling stories about money. The problem is many women's stories keep them (and their listeners) stuck in one view of reality, without providing openings for the possibility of change. We connect around our sense of victimhood, our ineptitude, and fears. It's easy to find other women who will identify with our difficulties and validate our fears. Then we can continue to live inside our stories, as if they were the only objective, factual truth.

It is as though we look at money through a lens that distorts the reality. The phrase "Money Mystique" refers to the idea that women often think of money as a mysterious, rather intimidating, and distinctly unfeminine medium. They relate to money as if is a bewildering, arcane subject that they can't be expected to understand. Moreover, they have the idea that they don't even need to understand money because someone else will take care of that part of their lives for them.

When you can see through the veil of the money mystique, you can also see that the story you tell yourself about your relation to money is just one possibility for you. There are other stories you could tell yourself about money that also might be true. Separating your actual experiences from your interpretations about the role that money has played in your life may seem like an odd first step to take toward managing your money. But I think the process is accomplished the same way that any change is: subtle, internal shifts are the source of big, external results. It reminds me of how turning a little rudder will alter the course of a large ship. Changing your relationship with money is a big undertaking. Examining the stories you tell yourself about money and separating the facts from the fictions is a small, effective first step.

Think About It . . .

Now, get your journal, sketchpad, and any other tools you might need to do this exercise. Give yourself time to consider the following questions. Then write, draw, doodle, or make diagrams, but do whatever works best for you to explore your answers:

- *How do you talk with yourself and others about money? What stories do you tell? How do you feel when you think about money?*

- *Remember the last few conversations you had about money. What was "the truth" or "the way it was" for you?*

- *When you think or talk about money, are your stories set in the past, present, or future?*

- *Is money your friend? Or is it a tool? Is money an enemy?*

- *Is money an annoyance? Or a joy?*

- *In your ideal world, would money exist? If so, how would you use it? Why is this not an ideal world?*

It All Begins with a Thought

Everything in creation first existed as a thought. The more specific the thought, the more powerful the creation. We think and we create. Everybody does it. It's impossible not to. We create amazing meals from raw food. We create crops that we put through machines to turn raw fiber into cloth and entire wardrobes. We create jobs and careers and businesses and industries. We create relationships and families and children and legacies. We create problems and we create solutions.

We create something every minute. While you are reading this sentence, you are creating a new reality, another piece to add to your familiar reality, or perhaps something in between. You create an opinion, a judgment, and a place to fit this new piece in with the other pieces. Or you create a blockage, or a barrier: "No new data allowed." You create your reality with your thoughts and shape it moment to moment. Whether you think of yourself as "creative" or "stuck in a rut," you're always creating your reality for yourself, all day long, every single day.

I believe that our experiences are inherently neutral. They're not "good" or "bad." They just are. You give your life form and richness by the meanings and interpretations you assign to your experiences. You literally color your world with your thoughts and beliefs. Perception becomes reality. You can't stop it. It's automatic—human beings transform experience into meaning as easily and automatically as toddlers turn the sounds they hear into recognizable speech.

You Experience Your Expectations

Now, here's an interesting twist. Not only do you color your experience with your beliefs, but your beliefs also determine the range of experiences you can have. You limit the range of what is possible by what you believe. You can't venture outside the parameters of your beliefs without creating turbulence. So you may try to stay inside the lines. That's the path of least resistance, the easiest one to follow.

You experience life as you believe you will experience it. You expect what you get, and you get what you expect. You do this whether you intend to or not. We all do it. We can't help it. We are spin doctors, always telling our stories, based on our beliefs and the beliefs of our friends and families. If you believe that life is hard, then life is hard. If you believe that money is difficult to come by, then that is your reality. If you believe people are kind and generous, you will experience them that way. It just happens. The mind can create only within the range that you, consciously or subconsciously, allow it to examine.

That is why it is so important to examine your own mind, to understand yourself, and to get rid of unwanted beliefs or habits. Otherwise, you are at risk of operating from beliefs you don't want, creating and re-creating a life you would not consciously choose. When you make a habit of consciously examining and choosing your beliefs, especially your beliefs about money, you move yourself into position to create your life and tell yourself the stories you want to be true. You become the captain of your own life, and you can take the ship anywhere you want to go.

As children, we learned about money the same way we learned about everything else—by observing the world around us. For most of us, that world consisted primarily of the adults in our lives, other kids, the media (particularly television), and school. Of all these, I think the behavior of adults has the greatest influence on how children relate to money when they grow up. For better or worse, adults are their role models. It is natural for families, and indeed societies, to pass their beliefs and values on to each new generation. It's part of helping the next generation make sense of the world in the way that best fits the group. Typically, we carry what we learned as children into our adult lives. We continue the legacy. This is particularly true when it comes to the family's story about money.

Our childhood stories, which are often gleaned more by observation than by direct participation in our family's finances, form the foundation of our ideas and beliefs about money as adults. Most of the time we're not even aware of what we inherited. Unquestioned, our beliefs are given free reign. Unexamined, they can wreak havoc in our lives.

For example, you may have been raised in a family where there was never enough money. So you grew up with the idea that there is never enough, and indeed, that is your experience. Or perhaps you grew up in a family where money was used to demonstrate love. In this case, you probably equate money with love and find it difficult to separate the two. Or maybe you learned that money creates conflict, so you choose to steer clear of dealing with money at all. Your unconscious credo might be summed up as, "Ignore money, no conflict."

 Think About It . . .

> *Whatever your situation, you will benefit by examining your story. Dig around inside. Take out your journal and prepare to answer the following questions. Give yourself time to think about these matters. Ask yourself:*

- *What are my assumptions about money?*

- *Where have I been with the money in my life? Where am I now?*

- *Do my beliefs about money serve me now? How did they serve me earlier in my life?*

- *What is automatically, unquestionably true for me—about my life and, specifically, about money in my life?*

- *Does my experience match what I expect life to be?*

- *What did my family teach me, intended or not, about money? What childhood impressions do I still believe? What ideas do I want to pass on to the next generation?*

Assumptions About Money

As you begin to explore the stories you tell yourself about money, you'll find you have certain basic, unspoken, unexamined assumptions. You might believe it is a scarce and limited resource, something only other people have. Or you may think you can have anything you want—money is not an obstacle. You might think money is security, or that it creates strife and misery. There is a huge range of possibilities. It is important to understand that there are no "right" or "wrong" assumptions. Many of your assumptions about money may serve you very well. Keep those and discard the rest.

Your assumptions about money directly relate to how successful you are in meeting your goals. They can propel you forward or they can hold you back. Understanding your core thoughts and beliefs about money is the only way to make lasting changes. When you bring your assumptions out of the shadows and into conscious awareness, they no longer control you. You are free to assess what works and what doesn't. You will be able to neutralize the power that money has over your life. You will be able to identify the distinction between money and how it is used.

Money itself is just a means to an end. The means to any number of ends. Money is a tool you can use to bring whatever you want into your life. You can bring comfort into your life. You can help the people you love. You can help humanity at large. Money is amazing. It is both a creation in itself and a catalyst for further creation.

As you explore your thoughts, beliefs, and assumptions about money, you'll develop the ability to feel a variety of emotions about it and still remain centered. You can have the awareness of emotions such as panic or fear without needing to act irrationally because of those emotions. You can feel the feeling and keep moving forward . . . reach the next level of awareness, and make the next choice. When you stay conscious, and detached, you'll get what you want—without the drama. One woman who went through this process described it as "grace." Imagine that . . . grace around money. Sound nice? It is. However, be forewarned. There is work involved. It is difficult to examine your family programming. Self-examination can be a harrowing process. Questioning your past can be frightening. It takes courage to step outside of the family consciousness to create your own consciousness.

In some cases, family members may balk. They may want you to stay where you are—with them. People like it when you agree with their version of your story. It can be threatening to question their version of reality. Anyone challenging the family story runs the risk of creating friction. Change can be frightening for you and everyone around you. In other cases, family members are simply oblivious to what is really happening within the family circle. In these families, some women are just not seen, even if they are going through the most monumental internal shifts.

Whatever your situation, I encourage you to take a deep breath, summon your courage and dive in. Examine your past, look at where you are right now, and lay yourself a strong foundation for your tomorrows. The rewards are worth it.

Making Judgments

I use the terms "rich" and "poor" without definition. It is impossible for me to know how you perceive those words. Everyone's ideas are different. They're completely subjective and relative terms. What is "rich" for one woman means "poor" for another. This inability to arrive at a common definition of two of the most overworked terms in our language is a great example of how our assumptions about money work.

 Think About It . . .

> *Define rich and poor for yourself. In your journal, explore your answers to these questions:*

- *List the people you know whom you believe are rich. How do you know they are rich? You may think they are rich; do you also believe that they think they are rich?*

- *How can you tell when people are poor? By the clothes they wear? By the car they drive, or the house they live in?*

- *Ask your friends about their definitions of rich and poor. You will be amazed at the variety of answers you get.*

"Rich People Are Bad!"

One common assumption I often hear about money is that there is something wrong with those who have it, that having money is somehow shameful. The underlying belief is that those who have money don't have good values. I hear many people who, by their own definitions don't have much money, make frequent negative judgments against those who do have money.

For example, once I was talking to a woman who had just landed the job of her dreams. She was a corporate consultant, and she had won an assignment to work with senior executives at a national retail chain. She was delighted with her new assignment until she finished her first day on the job. She told me, "I can't work with those people. They make more than $100,000 a year." I asked, "Why is that a problem?" She replied, "They don't have the same values I do. I just can't relate to them."

Then I asked her how she could identify their values by their salaries. I also asked her how much money she had made the previous year. "$24,000" was her answer. I then asked her, "If these executives made $24,000 instead of $100,000, would that be proof that they have the same values you do?" She had to think before she answered, "I don't know."

Somewhere in her mind she had separated herself from those she perceived as wealthy. She tenaciously held on to her belief that rich people aren't as "good" as she is. Operating unconsciously, this belief actually keeps her at the lower end of the income scale. She was having a hard time getting by and had no money to invest for her future. Yet clearly she felt virtuous in defending her assumptions about poverty as morally superior to wealth.

There is no valor in poverty. Abraham Lincoln said, "The best thing you can do for poor people is not be one of them." Like rich people, poor people come in all variations—generous and stingy, mean-spirited and kindly, thrifty and extravagant. The difference isn't in the money: it's in the person and the meaning he or she assigns to money.

"Rich People Are Good!"

People are just people. It is true, of course, that one of the benefits of having money is that you are in a position to help others. Rich people support the arts, sciences, and education. Lorenzo di Medici, the Italian statesman, supported artists like Leonardo da Vinci and Michelangelo and the Italian Renaissance was born. The wonderful music of Bach, Mozart, and Brahms was supported by rich patrons. Columbus' voyages to the new world were supported by the Queen of Spain. Where would we be if Queen Isabella had thought she didn't deserve to have money?

Andrew Carnegie built the system of free public libraries that we take for granted in the U.S. Paul Mellon devoted his life to creating the National Gallery of Art in Washington, D.C. Go to a museum, attend a symphony, and honor the names on the wall plaques or in the programs of those people and companies who made it possible for you to enjoy your experience.

You can do a lot of good in the world if you create wealth. You don't need enormous wealth to contribute. Many people of very modest means help others. They donate their time, talent, and money as they can.

Think About It ...

How many people in your community support the arts, theater, children's programs, and other charitable causes? Are they rich? What is their motivation? What can you learn from them? Do you want to be like them or not? Do you have a particular idea or cause that you want to support financially? How can you do this?

The "Victim"

Another assumption about money I like to challenge is that of being the victim. "If it weren't for (fill in the blank . . . my husband, my father, my boss, my children, taxes, etc.) I would be fine." The victim assumes no financial responsibility for herself and the choices she makes. She feels defeated before she gets out of bed in the morning. She knows it doesn't matter what she does; she won't succeed anyway. Nothing she does makes a difference. She is a victim and she can't do anything about it. Her absolute belief in her victimhood is a basic part of her identity. How could her life possibly be different? She's set the outer limit, and she stays inside her story.

I also see a subtler form of identifying as a victim in women who believe they cannot earn much money. They slightly resent having to deal with earning money. These are bright, capable, hardworking women. But they don't ever seem to get ahead. Their limiting beliefs prevent them from enjoying the success they say they want. They feel angry and defeated with a world that doesn't reward them very well. Their anger colors every aspect of their lives. But they feel powerless. They are victims, living in a world of scarcity. They truly believe there is never enough, that life isn't fair and that somebody else got their share. Worse yet, they believe they can't do anything about it. They will remain stuck as long as they hold on to their belief in their own powerlessness.

Listening to Yourself

It is imperative that you listen to your internal dialogue about money. Look for familiar refrains. Watch out for "I can't earn money" or "I can't take care of myself." "I can't" messages become self-fulfilling prophecies. If you believe them, they're true. If you believe you can't take care of yourself, you can't. It doesn't matter how educated you are, or how motivated. If you expect to fail, you will unconsciously sabotage your attempts to succeed.

If you tell yourself you are in control of your life and you trust your intuition, you will live with equanimity. If you believe that money circulates and that there is enough for everyone, you will not be fearful about money. The smallest shift in your awareness offers instant benefits. Of course, you have to take positive actions as well. Remember, beliefs and behaviors create results.

Inheriting Isn't the Answer

If you think everything would be just great if you only had more money, challenge that idea. I've talked with many women who inherited wealth, and I've heard them give voice to negative beliefs—about themselves and about money. Some believe they can't earn money. Or that there is never enough money. Some feel they don't deserve money. Others, ashamed to have plenty of money for life's pleasures, feel shamed by their friends who have more limited resources, so they try to hide their wealth.

These women really believe their stories. When we explore their situation a little further, we discover they have an underlying belief that prevents them from using their inheritance with a sense of purpose. They are afraid they will squander the money and then they will be destitute. They believe they can't manage their money properly. And they believe they can't earn it themselves. If you are on the outside looking in on their lives, their feelings might surprise you.

Such women become the victims of their fears. I've seen women of inherited wealth burn through it. This confirmed the story they told themselves that they can't handle money. I've also seen women with plenty of money lead small, scared lives—afraid to touch the money, let alone spend or invest it. I see many women who leave hundreds of thousands of dollars in money market accounts, with very low returns, because they are too afraid to invest in the stock market. They are afraid to bear the consequences of being in control. Yet they don't want to give up their perceived control and hire a financial advisor to help them.

I worked with one savvy young woman for a year. She came to see me because she wanted to change her mind about money. At thirty-eight, she had a net worth of more than $5 million. Yet she lived in constant terror that the money would go away. She did not trust herself. She had three basic assumptions. She believed she didn't deserve the money. She believed she didn't know and could not learn how to manage the money. And she believed the money would disappear, and she wouldn't be able to support herself when it was gone. Because of these beliefs she didn't trust her money in the stock market. She kept her entire inheritance in Treasury bills. Her lack of investment knowledge made her feel even more at risk. People told her she needed to invest, but she was afraid. She was afraid to invest and she was afraid not to invest.

From the time she was very young, she had known that she was going to inherit a fortune from her uncle. She was told she would never have to work or worry about money. She became a perpetual student. She had one undergraduate degree and two advanced degrees. But she never used her education to pursue a career. Even though she didn't actually inherit the money until she was thirty-two, her belief that she couldn't earn money was so strong it never occurred to her that she could support herself. She always knew the inheritance was coming. So she worked at marginal jobs when she wasn't in school. When the jobs became tedious, she went back to school for another degree. But she never took a finance class. She thought it would be too boring. When we examined this a bit closer, what she really believed was that she wouldn't be able to understand finance. And she didn't want to risk embarrassment or failure.

Her personal life was a string of failed romances. She repeatedly chose to partner with men who lived on the economic edge. She believed they loved her only for her money, so she couldn't fully commit. She felt great sadness about not having children. To the casual observer, this woman appears to have it made. She doesn't have to work. She is taken care of. She is an easy target for other women who envy her wealth. She is the proverbial "poor little rich girl." But, internally, she feels isolated and afraid.

I met with another woman, also in her late thirties, who had a very different story about money. She and her sisters had always "known" they would inherit when their grandfather died. It was a common family assumption. Her mother and grandmother always told her she never had to worry about money. The story she learned was that she would be taken care of for her entire life.

The reality turned out quite different from the family story. When the grandfather died, the truth came out. Everybody in the family inherited their rightful shares, several million dollars each. That is, everyone except my client. Her grandfather had held a grudge against her from the time she was a child. He punished her by stipulating that she couldn't inherit her share until she turned sixty. He had never told anyone about his grudge, or the little bombshell in his will. My client is approaching mid-life. She has no job, no job prospects, and no money.

She never really wanted to work for a living. No one else in her family worked. When she was younger, she had been taught that she would never have to work. In fact, her mother supported her for years while she waited for her inheritance. They both thought the inheritance would be large enough that she could pay her mother back.

This woman lived her entire life with a family promise that didn't come true. Now, here she was, on her own for the first time. She was going to have to fend for herself. She believed that she couldn't earn money. Her deeper feeling was that she shouldn't have to earn money. The idea of supporting herself was preposterous. It had never occurred to her that she could be self-supporting. It was an impossible idea.

She, too, had had several stormy relationships with men, and never married. She had a young daughter whom she adored. She felt ashamed that her daughter might discover that she couldn't take care of them. She felt angry and victimized, yet she was determined to take control of her life. She was willing to do everything she could to take care of herself.

I encouraged both of these women to honestly explore their ideas about money. They both kept journals where they jotted down the ideas about money that occurred to them. We examined the patterns in their thoughts. They were surprised to see how many times the same thoughts surfaced. Their self-talk was a constant barrage of negativity. "I deserve to be taken care of." "I can't earn money." The cacophony was deafening. They were driving themselves crazy.

I am pleased to report that the first woman was very successful in building a new framework for thinking about money. We worked together for about a year. She was ready to change her mind and willing to do the work. She was able to look at her beliefs, and kept what worked and got rid of what didn't. She worked very hard to get where she is today. For the first time in her life, she is working in a field that shows promise as a career. She is slowly learning about investing and the stock market. She takes more risks with her money and in her life. She still gets a little scared but knows the fear will pass.

My other client made modest progress before she gave up. She continues to live in the world of "life isn't fair" and "I don't want to take care of myself." She isn't yet willing to complete the arduous process of growing up and relating to the world as a mature woman. She has found a man to provide for her instead.

I encourage wealthy parents to be very careful about leaving their money to their children. If children grow up believing someone else will always take care of them, they often remain weak and child-like. Of course, it isn't the money that weakens a child; it's the attitude about the money.

Children need to know that the power, responsibility, and ability to care for themselves reside within themselves, not in money. When girls are told they are smart and strong and capable of taking care of themselves, they grow up that way, with or without inherited money. If there is money in the family, it just makes their life better. It doesn't make their life.

Money Is Hard to Ignore

It isn't possible to be happy and ignore the role of money in your life. In the United States, as in all market economies, it takes money to get your needs met. Like it or not, there isn't any other way. You can balk at the system, or you can learn to understand it and make it work for you. It is up to you.

You can learn to be friendly with money by changing the way you talk about it. When you think a negative thought about money, examine it immediately. Is your thought original, or is it something you learned as you were growing up? How does this negative thought help you? Reframe your negative feelings and thoughts so they take on a positive tone. You may need to be extremely watchful at first, negative thoughts are persistent. It takes commitment, patience, and practice to change a habit. But the freedom you'll feel as you transform your relationship with money is worth the effort.

When you challenge yourself in this way, you not only challenge your present, but also your past. You are stepping into uncharted waters. Many women find a familiar comfort in their negative ideas about money. It can be daunting to move into new beliefs.

When you no longer have attitudes that are self-defeating, you have to take more responsibility. This is no small matter. You are exchanging your unhealthy relationship to money for a healthy one. But it is unknown—and the unknown can be frightening at times.

Words Make a Difference

Listen to yourself when you talk about money, to yourself and others. Be very careful in your language. Identify and name your ideas. You create your reality with every word you say and every thought you think. Women who assume responsibility for themselves and tell themselves they can provide for themselves create the money in their lives, *because they believe they can.*

When a woman realizes the creative capacity of her own consciousness, when she can see her filters, choose or change her beliefs, and assume responsibility for herself, she wakes up. She becomes more powerful than she ever thought she could be. It's a wonderful experience, one I've had the honor of witnessing many times. There's a magical moment when you see that someone "gets it." When a woman really understands that she creates her reality, and realizes that she can create it anyway she likes. The only "string" attached is that she must be responsible for herself. I've seen many women embrace this shift. Amazing, inspiring, "ordinary" women. They do it one day at a time. Just as you do.

CHAPTER THREE

THE ONLY THING YOU HAVE TO CHANGE IS YOUR MIND

Progress is impossible without change, and those who cannot change their minds cannot change anything.

George Bernard Shaw (1856–1950)

Learning to manage change gracefully can make your life easier. Nothing stays the same from one minute to the next. Change is always present. The biggest challenge you face is adjusting to change easily and happily. If you can do that, it means you are able to see when a change has occurred and you can change your ideas to correspond with it, so that you stay current. You cannot live in the present if you don't adjust to the changes in your life. And living in the present, as opposed to living in the past—or the future—is essential for a satisfying life.

 Think About It ...

In your journal, draw lines to create separate columns. Each column should be labeled as a decade in your life. For

example, your first column will be from zero to ten years of age. The second column will be for ten through twenty and so forth. Be sure to leave some columns blank to fill in future decades yet to come.

- *Write down your life experiences in decades. Start from when you were born to age ten, then think about your life from age ten to twenty. Do this for each ten-year period up to the present. Notice how your life circumstances changed in that time. Think about ways you would have managed change differently given the advantage of hindsight. What were your greatest challenges with change? What were your greatest successes with change?*

- *Now, think and write about the rest of your life in ten-year increments. How will your life be different in ten years than it is today? In twenty years? How are you going to manage those changes and remain steady and grounded?*

- *Now write your own eulogy. What do you want people to remember about you? What is your legacy?*

If you are thinking about your life and how you want it to be, you are in a great place to examine the everyday details. For example, a few years ago I reconsidered my need to celebrate Christmas the way I always had. Usually, I put up a tree, decorated the house, purchased gifts, and joined in all the hoopla. However, a year finally arrived when I felt unenthusiastic about the whole ritual. I felt a little anxious and guilty that I wasn't excited, but the plain truth was I didn't want to participate in my usual way. Things had changed.

When I was married with small children, the holidays were a big deal for all of us. Now I am single and I live by myself. I realized that nobody was forcing me to celebrate holidays in the traditional way. I adopted an every other year plan. I participate wholeheartedly in the festivities one year and take the following year off.

I have used this approach for several years now, and I love it. On the "off" year I make little effort to decorate. Instead, I appreciate everyone else's decorations. Other people put up beautiful decorations. I had never really noticed that previously because I was focused on doing my own thing. Once again, I love Christmas. I think I enjoy the "off" years better than the "on" years. What I love most is knowing that I can choose how I want to celebrate the holidays, and anything else in my life.

Think About It . . .

> *As your life changes, try to be willing to change your beliefs about what you need to be happy. Sometimes it takes a while to figure out a new approach. Whenever you start feeling anxious about a habit, a ritual, or anything in your life, question yourself. Spend time alone to write in your journal, draw, take a walk, or talk with a friend. Anxiety, while uncomfortable, is also your ally. It is your inner voice talking to you. Listen, explore the anxiety, and see what there is to learn.*
>
> *Often our anxieties move us to make changes. Are there any changes you want to make? Any habits to replace, rituals to reconsider or choices to make? Are your choices rooted to the past, the present, or the future?*

When you challenge your ideas and beliefs about your life and your money (the two go together!), you may surprise yourself. It can be quite a wonderful experience. Consider the power you have when you realize that you don't have to remain attached to beliefs that no longer serve you. It's exciting. It is also exciting to recognize and understand the beliefs that still work for you. Remember the world isn't black and white. You will love knowing what you want to change and what you want to keep.

Waking Up, Gently

I encourage you to take an unemotional, nonjudgmental appraisal of your relationship with money. Be forgiving of yourself. Dismiss shame and guilt if they appear. These negative emotions are not constructive. In fact, they can be damaging. Too often, shame and guilt stop women from continuing the process of taking a complete appraisal of their relationship with money, once they have started it. If you feel your emotions rising, be very gentle with yourself. You didn't pull your money behaviors out of thin air. You learned them. If they don't serve you anymore, you can change them. It is a waste of your precious life energy to sit in harsh judgment of anything, especially yourself.

$ Think About It . . .

Gently observe your thinking and behaviors around money. In your journal, write down your actions and why you think you act the way you do. If you observe unhealthy patterns, you will probably want to change them. It is empowering to discover old patterns that have been hidden from view. Self-understanding gives you the ability to make positive changes, step by step, day by day. Write down a few actions you can take to change your behavior patterns with money.

Making Connections

Deborah came to see me because she was feeling anxious about her money. It didn't take her long to see that she spends way too much money on clothes and personal adornments. While we were examining her thinking and behavior around shopping, she made a connection that stunned her. She was following in her mother's foot-steps, and had never seen it before. Her mother also had spent more money than was appropriate on Deborah's clothing. Her mother had been very focused on Deborah's "looking nice." As a "good" daughter, Deborah believed it was her duty to have a large closet full of beautiful clothes. She had never even questioned this particular need. The problem was that her clothing purchases were both excessive and inappropriate. At age forty-five, she should have been more focused on investing and taking care of her future. What's more, she was using credit cards to pay for her purchases. It is no wonder she felt anxious most of the time.

Deborah was thrilled to discover the connection between her current financial situation (high anxiety) and her automatic thinking and behaviors. She appreciates her mother's point of view, but she wants to live differently. Now that she knows where her behavior originated, she will be successful in making the changes she wants. She has changed her mind. New behaviors will follow. Now she can reap the rewards of having examined her life. She can have the life she consciously chooses. These simple acts of noticing, questioning, and making connections will make a big difference in Deborah's daily experience of life, and in her long-term financial success.

Deborah's story is a fairly common one. I have observed that when women spend too much money, it's often spent on clothing and personal items. Why? One answer is that we live in a society where women are valued for their appearance. For many people, looking good to others is of the utmost importance. Often, we learned this from our mothers, and we carry on the legacy, without questioning it. We mother ourselves the same way we were mothered.

Baby Steps

It's glorious when a woman wakes up to herself. The world changes right before her eyes. She gradually realizes she is free to release old ideas and beliefs that don't work for her. The confusion lifts. There is less struggle. She begins to feel confident in her own choices, choices that support her where she is right now. She doesn't feel guilty about changing. She feels free, perhaps for the first time in her life.

It's not difficult. It is a process of baby steps. A little change here. A little change there. Challenge your habits and thought patterns as you go. You can change your entire future by changing your thoughts just a little. This is particularly true when dealing with money. It doesn't take a big change of mind to result in a big change of experience. Once you begin to see things a bit differently, you move into a comfort zone where you can experience freedom and success.

Getting to Know Your Comfort Zone

Your comfort zone is the unconscious perimeter you construct around yourself. It helps you make sense of your world. You need it because you would go crazy if you didn't have a framework for being in the world. That's because you think uncountable numbers of thoughts in a day. You encounter hundreds of thousands of stimuli and distractions. You build your framework to make sense of everything that goes on around you. You build it little by little, day by day, as you grow and observe life around you. It is comprised of items you learn at home, at school, and from the culture at large.

You create a comfort zone about every facet of your life. You like to live in a certain kind of house. You are comfortable driving a particular type of car. You like associating with people who are like you. Over time, you place a great deal of value on your beliefs. You feel very comfortable with the view from your particular frame of reference. Your mind becomes set without your being conscious of it. You may sincerely value keeping an open mind, but it is difficult to do because of the challenging circumstances you face every day. The familiarity of your life is both a comfort, and a trap.

It is human nature to believe that your framework is reality. Human beings constantly look for evidence that affirms our point of view. But changing your mind creates anxiety. Change moves you out to the edge of your comfort zone. Of course, this all happens at an unconscious level. If you live in a comfort zone that says you have to work hard for money, you may continually seek evidence to prove this point. On the other hand, if you believe life is easy and there is enough money for you and everyone else, that is probably what your experience has been. You'll see evidence of your point of view every place you look. You will discount evidence that does not match your unconscious beliefs. When you see concrete evidence that your opinion is not valid, you may discount it with excuses, or call it a fluke. That is human nature.

I am amazed at how this process manifests in my own life. I do not want to live unconsciously in a comfort zone that I don't really want. I try to live as consciously as I can. This has been one of my biggest challenges. Every year or so, I examine every single habit I have. I review the route I take to work, where I go to lunch, the movies I see, the friends I spend time with, the money I spend, what I read—everything.

Just a Cup of Coffee

For example, I used to go to Starbucks for coffee nearly every weekday. I never questioned the habit. I love the coffee and I enjoy the atmosphere. But when I examined my Starbucks experience closely, it left a lot to be desired. I usually had to drive out of my way to get there. I parked in a crowded parking lot only to wait in a long line to place my order. Then I had to wait in the same long line to get my coffee to go. I have a cup holder in my car, but three times out of five, the coffee would spill as I made a turn. I actually carried a towel in my car just for coffee spills! Then I would carry the coffee to my office, set it down on my desk, and never drink it. I would get busy working and forget about it. When I remembered, it was usually cold. I was not having many sublime coffee experiences.

Once I examined this pattern, I changed it. Now I go to Starbucks for a special treat, when I have lots of time and I can drink it there. I meet friends for coffee sometimes, which is nice. I've also noticed the savings have added up. I spend much less on coffee by making it at home and carrying it to work in a thermos. And the best news is that it's always hot when I drink it.

 Think About It . . .

> *In your journal, jot down your ideas for managing the changes in your life. Are you struggling with something? How can you make it feel easier? What is your comfort zone with money? Where did you pick up your feelings about money? Do you want to continue living in this comfort zone or would you like to expand your horizons? How can you do this?*

A Radical Notion

You can't make significant changes in your comfort zone until you know what your comfort zone is. If you are going to change your mind, you need to understand what you think (and maybe even why). You need to examine your framework about money. It is so easy to just go along day after day doing what you do without ever really thinking about it. Sometimes I suggest to clients that they change in rather dramatic ways. We end up laughing, because as a rule the required change is rather obvious, but they hadn't ever considered it.

For example, Jane had always carried credit card balances. In her life, debt was an unquestioned fact, a way of life. It never occurred to her to pay them off, even though she had the money to do so. She gave me a very puzzled look when I suggested she pay off her credit card balances. She didn't know whether to laugh or cry. We both burst out laughing at the power of her resistance. It took her about two weeks to get used to the idea and actually pay off all the balances. Today, she can't even imagine that she used to carry debt. Now that she's not buying interest (which really means buying nothing), her money goes for the things she truly wants.

Creatures of Habit

We have habits for good reasons. Many habits are developed because they support our lives. For example, you buckle your seat belt when you drive, you floss your teeth, you watch the news. You observe many of these habits without having to think about them.

They serve you well. Some habits are worth keeping. Some are not. Examine your thoughts, beliefs, and actions in any areas of your life that are not working. If everything is working beautifully and you feel in control and powerful in your life, great. But, if there is anything in your life you would like to change, examining your thoughts is the place to begin.

Stuck in the Struggle

If you struggle with money, the chances are good that you do not understand why you struggle. You may ask yourself, "Why does it have to be so hard?" You may say you don't want to struggle anymore. You know you want things to change. But, somehow, the struggle continues. The answer lies in the subtle trappings of your comfort zone. You won't be able to give up the struggle as long as you stay stuck in your belief system. As strange as this idea may seem to you, your struggle is comfortable—because it's what you know. It's not that you like the idea of struggle, but it is familiar. There is always some degree of comfort in what is known.

You build your comfort zone with money with the ideas you carry with you, ideas that are deeply imbedded in your unconscious mind. Understanding your comfort zone helps you to step outside of it, to challenge it, and to grow from the experience. Challenging your comfort zone allows you to expand and move in the direction you want to go. It allows you to break free from the stagnant patterns in your life. Challenging your comfort zone provides fresh air to breathe.

For example, you may not have the money to live the life you want. You may envy others for their seeming ease in getting what they want. However, if you examine your own comfort zone and compare it to another's, you will find they are different. Women who create the lives they want are willing to step out of their comfort zones. They are willing to move from the comfortable middle, where life is known, to the edge where change is constant. This takes courage.

Changing Yourself Changes Your Circumstances

Changing your financial picture is not enough to change yourself. Lottery winners provide a remarkable example of this. Many lottery winners are completely unable to break out of their comfort zones around money. This may seem odd, but it's true. One day they are scraping along struggling to make ends meet and the next day they have more than a million dollars. They think they are on easy street for the rest of their lives. But within a few short years, many of these people are right back where they started: living from paycheck to paycheck. Why? Because the money didn't change them, and they didn't change their comfort zones.

If you unconsciously step out of your comfort zone, you will unconsciously do everything possible to move right back into it. This works for both sides of the zone. That is, this is true for those who always expect to have enough money as well as for those who expect to never have enough.

For example, I know people who have lost everything because of illness or a failed business venture. But they live in an expanded comfort zone, so they have an abiding faith in their ability to recreate their comfortable financial circumstances. So they do, again and again. They can't fail because without money they are outside of their comfort zone. They just assume they will be "back in the money" in no time. Look around you at those who have the "golden touch." What is their comfort zone with money? Very likely they believe they will always have money.

Amy's Story

Amy, a twenty-five-year-old sales clerk, told me that she had been in a very serious automobile accident when she was sixteen. Two years later, she was awarded a judgment of $400,000, which made her and her parents ecstatic. They believed their ship had come in and they could have everything they had always wanted. Amy bought two houses, one for her mother and another for her father and his new wife. She bought expensive cars for everybody in the family, six in all. When she went clothes shopping, she was as generous with her friends as she was with herself.

In eighteen months, all of the money was gone. By the time she was twenty, Amy was penniless. She had a nice car, but that was it. Her friends dispersed after high school. Her mother couldn't keep up the payments and lost her house. And Amy reproaches herself every single day. She said, "I had all that money and now I make about $18,000 a year. How can I ever get it back?"

She ended her story by telling me that Jason, the boy who was with her in the car accident, is now a millionaire. He manages his money full-time. At the age of twenty-five he is financially set for life.

I asked her what made the difference between her and Jason. She answered immediately and said, "Our parents. His parents said he could have a new car, but that was it. They insisted that he invest the rest of the money. On the other hand, my parents couldn't wait to spend my money."

Ron's Story

I heard a similar story when I ran into a colleague, Ron, who said, "I've been meaning to call you, but now it's too late. I inherited quite a bundle when my cousin died last year. I was going to ask you how to invest it, but now it's almost gone. I spent it. I probably shouldn't have, but it's been so much fun. I bought two new Jaguars, one for me and one for my wife. We bought a huge new house that we just love. We've had a blast with my cousin's money!"

I asked Ron if his cousin had been a wealthy woman. He replied, "Oh, heavens no! Nobody in my family is wealthy. My cousin scrimped and saved all her life so she could pass on a legacy." As I drove home, I wondered if Ron's use of the money resembled his aunt's idea of a legacy.

Both Amy and Ron operate from a comfort zone where they don't have money. Both of them exchanged all of their money for consumer goods. They didn't put any money aside so it could grow for the future. Now it's very likely that they will always have to work for money because they don't have money working for them. If they'd had a different comfort zone, if they had thought about tomorrow, they could have had money working for them today.

Accept the Challenge

It takes real commitment to alter your thinking and change your mind. As you try to change, people may refuse to support you. They will tell you it is impossible for you to succeed. They will tell you that failure is right around the corner. When you hear negative comments about actions you believe will be positive forces in your life, listen with an open heart. Recognize that these people feel challenged themselves. They aren't really talking about you, they're talking about themselves.

Susan's Story

Susan is a top pilot for an international airline. She's managed to live her life by being true to herself, and it has really paid off. She always wanted to be a pilot. She began her training back in the days when women didn't fly planes. Men flew planes and women served coffee. But she never wavered. In spite of many naysayers, she earned her pilot's wings. It took her some time before a small, local company hired her. It wasn't too many years before she was flying nationally. Now she flies internationally. She has a great job at a fine salary and a good pension. She would never have realized her dream if she hadn't been willing to challenge her comfort zone, and the comfort zones of the many people who thought women should stay in their place.

It takes courage to move to the edge and step off without knowing where the bottom is. You alternate between feelings of euphoria and panic. Some people just can't take the pressure, and jump right back into the comfortable middle. Often, there is a part of you that wants to change, and a part of you that doesn't. Sometimes the part that doesn't want to change wins the first round, but you always have the final decision.

Change Your Mind About Changing Your Mind

If you don't think you can change your mind, change your mind about changing your mind! Make changing your mind easy. Don't think of it as something *more* to do. Think of it as something *less* to do. Changing your mind can be really fun, if you let it be. Lighten up. Breathe. Laugh about it.

Be gentle with yourself. The hardest part about examining your comfort zone is understanding your present circumstances and granting yourself permission to feel okay. Don't dwell on where you are and what's wrong. Focus on where you want to be and what is already working. Energy follows thought. The next time you're in a familiar situation, expecting a familiar outcome, change your expectation. Play with it, and see what happens. You might surprise yourself.

 Think About It . . .

It can be difficult to challenge your comfort zone and not feel shame or guilt. You may wish you hadn't made the life choices you've made so far. Please, don't beat yourself up. Focus on where you want to be. Gently look at your life, and

take actions today to move yourself out of a comfort zone you don't like and into a comfort zone that truly supports you. The more you learn about yourself and money, the easier it is to expand your comfort zone.

Chapter Four

It's Nice to Want

Energy rightly applied can accomplish anything.
Nellie Bly (1864–1922)

When my children were growing up and they told me they wanted things, I would respond with "It's nice to want." This is true. Wanting is a natural part of human nature. Of course you want to have things, experiences, and love. There is nothing wrong with wanting. It is a means of expressing yourself in the physical world. Wanting is important. We all want different things. No two people are alike. The trick is to determine your individual goals and dreams and figure out how to bring them into reality. Figuring it out involves the four steps outlined below.

1. **Desire.** You must first know exactly what it is you want. To do this, you must determine the *essence* of your desire. The essence of your desire is the part that brings out the best in you. It touches you to your very core. You want something because of the feeling it gives you—perhaps the feeling is satisfaction, or peace of mind, or joy. Suppose you say you want to be debt-free. The essence of being debt-free is financial freedom. You want financial freedom because your debt creates anxiety and fear of the future. This is in direct conflict with the essence of your desire to be financially free.

2. **Intention.** Once you know what you want, set a clear intention to bring your desire into reality. An intention is a desire that creates action. Without action you will not create your

desire. You must clearly state your intention to be debt-free. You might find it helpful to use an affirmation of your intention to send a strong message to the universe that this is your desire.

3. **Detach.** After you have made your affirmation you must give up any attachment to a specific outcome. Know that you'll receive this desire—or something better. Give up needing to control the process. Let go. Relax and allow the forces of the universe to work for you.

4. **Take action.** Give your attention to your intention. Do the work. Change your behaviors. Focus on the present. Stop trying to be debt-free. Be debt-free. Focus on doing the actions that will make your dreams come true rather than focusing on your dreams. This is how you give up attachment to the outcome. Focus on the moment and bring your goal into physical form.

Giving Your Vision Form

Every financial plan begins with the same questions: What do you want? What are your dreams and goals? How do you want your life to look in one year, five years, and twenty years? Do you see that these questions have nothing to do with money? "I want to have a million dollars" doesn't answer "What are your dreams and goals?" Neither does it describe how you want your life to be in the future. A million dollars might be useful for implementing a goal, assuming that you know what you want. Deciding what you would do with a million dollars can help you figure out what your goal is.

Money is relevant only when you know what you want to bring into your life. When you know that, then you are ready to gather together the resources you need to meet your goals. Furthermore, if you know what you want, you are very likely to get it. Everything that we human beings create first begins as an idea. The idea is transformed, through conscious intention and subsequent action, into a preliminary design, working model, a finished structure, whether it's a building or a college education. The idea always comes first. This is a universal principle. You may think that manifesting your dreams is an enormous challenge. But it doesn't necessarily have to be difficult. Try this on for size: Bringing a dream into reality is easy.

Desire and the Art of Manifesting

It all begins with desire. You have a desire, a want, a need, or a wish. First, you must focus on that desire. You must infuse it with energy. You must visualize having it. You will know what it looks like when it comes to you. The moment you decide what you want, you begin bringing it into your life. You don't have it yet, but you have started the process of getting it.

Find the Essence of Your Desire

Next, think about the *essence* of your desire. This will define it a little more clearly. You can determine what the essence of your desire is if you go deep inside and create in your imagination the feeling of actually having what you want. So, what is the essence of a desire? Well, suppose you are living in an inadequately heated home. You might say you want a furnace. Or you might wish you had a wood-burning stove. You might even say you want a fireplace. But what is the essence of what you really want? The answer is heat. Heat is the essence of your desire. Similarly, no matter what your specific desire is, it is important to distill it down to its essence.

 Think About It . . .

Now, take time to identify your desires and then look for their underlying essences. For example, suppose your desire is to live in a nicer place than where you currently reside. Close your eyes and imagine your perfect home. Don't worry about where the money will come from to pay for it. Don't think about money. Just try to visualize the details of your dream home. What does it look like? Is there a garden? How many rooms does it have? Visualize yourself in your favorite room, decorated with some of your favorite furnishings, and see yourself engaged in some pleasing activity in that room.

Now, visualize your specific desire. What does it feel like? Create an image of your desire and stay with the picture you create. Then focus on what it feels like to have what you want. Bask in the experience, as if you actually have whatever it is you want. What do you feel? It's the feeling that tells you when you are on the right track. You'll know when it feels right. In this exercise you want to stay inside the experience, not on the outside looking in.

The essence of your desire is contained in the feeling that arises when you imagine having what you want. The essence of desire isn't in the packaging. You can't think your way to it. And you can't force it. It's a feeling that comes to you. And it will come. You'll recognize it. It's a sense of deep satisfaction, and then some. It's the feeling you get when everything about that desire is perfect.

Have you ever had the experience of working on a project and having it all come together? And having everybody love your work? At that moment, you feel supremely competent and you know you are in the right place doing the right thing. That's the essence of yourself that you experience in that moment. In these moments you experience your fundamental nature. You are in contact with your innermost being.

Or suppose you want a relationship. You can imagine your perfect mate, the perfect date, your perfect life together. What is the feeling that comes up? Connection? Excitement? Serenity? Whatever emotional state would be perfect for you, whenever you hit the "A Hah!" moment, that's when you will know you have found the feeling and the essence of your desire.

Knowing What You Want

You may have a hard time deciding what you want because as a child you learned that you can't have what you want. You may have learned that you don't know what you want. Or you may believe you shouldn't want. Imagine this scenario: You are a child again. You go out shopping with a parent, and you ask for something. Your request is met with an angry scowl, and these words, "Do you think money grows on trees? You know we can't afford that!" Does this sound familiar? If you heard it often enough while you were growing up, you surely learned that you can't have what you want. Not surprisingly, as an adult, you believe that you can't have what you want. You are certain there isn't enough money. It may be a conscious or an unconscious belief, but it's there.

You may carry this belief with you for your entire life. It doesn't matter how much you actually have; it's never enough. I've met women with millions of dollars who don't believe there is enough money for them to have what they want. Interestingly, they don't try to help anybody else get what they want. They believe that there's never enough—for anyone.

This type of attitude really has very little to do with how much money is available. Their childhood feelings control these women's lives as surely as if they did not have enough money to pay their phone bills. As parents, women with these beliefs usually teach their children the same thing. These attitudes get passed on from generation to generation. It causes problems for the entire family. Often the family is in conflict because of money, and they aren't sure why. Their negative ideas and beliefs are deeply imbedded in the collective unconscious of the entire family system.

When Is Enough Enough?

Women who lived through the Great Depression of the 1930s or who were raised by parents who survived the Depression often have the feeling that there will never be enough. I once had a conversation with an eighty-one-year-old woman who needed a new car to replace her twenty-year-old vehicle. But she didn't think she could afford a brand-new one, even though she had several hundred thousand dollars in her portfolio. Our conversation went like this:

"Why can't you buy a new car?"

"Because I don't have enough money."

"You can buy a new car and have plenty of money left over to live."

"I would have to take the money from the principal and I'm not ever supposed to spend the principal."

"Why?"

"Because my father told me never to spend principal."

This woman had always lived modestly. She and her late husband diligently invested $50 a month, even though it had been a sacrifice. So I tried a different approach. I asked her, "What are you saving the money for? What would be a good use of your money?"

She answered, "It was supposed to be for our old age."

Curious, I asked, "When does old age begin?" This question caused her to pause. I continued, "If you don't consider eighty-one to be old age, what is? Eighty-five? Ninety? One hundred?" We both laughed.

Then she said, "What about leaving the money to my children?" I asked her if her children wanted her money. Her immediate answer was, "No."

I asked, "Do they need the money?"

"Not really," she said.

Then I gently asked her, "Why do you believe you are sacrificing today to leave your children money they do not want or need? Do you think they will love you more?"

"No."

"Will they think you love them more if you leave them your money?"

"No. They already know I love them."

"Then why not go ahead and buy a new car?" I said.

We hugged each other. She bought the car and absolutely loves it. Her children love it, too. They are very happy that she has started to enjoy the money she spent a lifetime saving. She is now reconsidering her position on spending her principal. It took her eighty-one years to believe there is enough money. We're still working on it. Just recently, she spent several hundred dollars on two beautiful purebred kittens. This may seem like a lot of money to spend on pets, but she adores her new housemates. They bring her joy every single day. She never thinks about how much they cost, because the benefit they have brought into her life cannot be measured in terms of dollars and cents.

Childhood Influences

As you can see, childhood events can set lifelong orientations about wanting and having. Another pattern I see frequently is that parents can thwart their children's desires by telling them they don't want what they think they want. The child will say, "I want that toy," and the parent replies, "No, you don't." Eventually, the child internalizes her parent's belief that she didn't want the toy. She grows up believing she doesn't know what she wants. Of course, she thought she wanted it at the time, but she reaches the conclusion that she must have been wrong. She believes her parent knows what she wants better than she does. As an adult, she transfers this belief to her husband or partner, to her friends or anyone outside of herself. She looks to others to determine what she wants.

She wants a dress exactly like the one her friend has. She wants a house like those she sees on television. She gives up her real identity. She gives up her heart's true longings. She wants what other people tell her she wants, either explicitly or implicitly.

Advertising

Nobody understands this dynamic better than advertisers. They believe most women are more anxious to fit in than to stand out from the crowd. They prey on the fact that women, for the most part, don't have well-developed egos and that they suffer from low self-esteem. Many ad campaigns direct their message to women's feelings of inadequacy. Furthermore, much of advertising is a subtle (and not so subtle) denigration of women. By telling us we will be slimmer if we drink their product, they assume we want or need to be slimmer. We buy into the fact that slim is the ideal, no matter what our body type. We become dissatisfied with our own bodies. This damages our psyche and our spirit. When you know what you want, you are immune to whatever Madison Avenue beams at you. Advertisers waste their time and money on you. You don't buy anything unless you truly want it. You don't need anyone to tell you what you want. You figure it out for yourself.

Children Get the Message

You are not the only one bombarded with thousands of advertising messages. Your children are deluged with them as well. As a parent or caregiver, you can stop the cycle of wanting everything for the wrong reasons. When your children ask for something, affirm their desire. Tell them it's okay to want things. Teach them that wanting something is a good enough reason to get it. Teach them they don't have to justify their desires. Their desire is enough.

But, at the same time, you must help them to make responsible choices. You may not want to buy the item for them right now. Your budget may not allow its immediate purchase, or a shopping trip may just not be feasible. But kids want what they want when they want it—and they need to learn that you can't always get what you want when you want it. Sometimes you have to wait. Tell them you don't want to buy it *today*. If they really want it, they can save or earn the money for it. Or, tell them you will buy it for them another day. Or they can have something else they want instead. Stay away from statements like "There isn't enough money to get it," or any other statements that send the message they can't have what they want. Your job is to help them figure out what they want and how to get it.

Pent-up Demands

This section wouldn't be complete without a discussion of timing. We live in the era of instant everything. It may be difficult to wait to get something. The ability to delay gratification of one's desires is a sign of maturity. It's also a statement of trust that the universe will provide. All things are received in their perfect time. It isn't for us to judge when the time is right. Our job is simply to express our desires and back them up with our behavior. Try keeping a "Pent-up Demand List." When you think of something you want, jot it down on the list. Trust that you will get it if it goes on the list. Using such a list will keep you from needing instant gratification.

Writing down what you want offers a lot of value in exchange for very little energy. When you write something on your list, you engage your mind and body. Writing sends a stronger message to the universe than if your idea is kept as just a thought. The written word is one step closer to physical reality than a thought. It is important, however, that once you have written a desire down, you must forget about it. You can let go of your attachment to the outcome because you know you will have it eventually—or something better. It's only a matter of time. Using a pent-up demand list frees your mind of clutter. Once it is on the list, it's out of your mind. Such a list can also keep you from buying things you don't want. In this way, you can learn to make more thoughtful choices.

Why Do You Buy What You Buy?

Some women buy things they don't really want. They buy because they are pressured, bored, or because the item is on sale. Buying something because it is on sale is not a good reason to buy it. It is much better to buy something you really want and pay full price. If you don't want something at full price, do you really want it at half price? Either you want it or you don't. Of course, if you find something you really want and it is on sale, that's great.

Women who shop sales can spend more money than women who buy things at full price. And, very often, they wind up with closets full of clothes they don't really love and want. Women who shop sales have a lot of tops and bottoms that don't go together. They live with huge amounts of stuff that has no meaning to them—stuff they bought only because it was sold at reduced prices. They keep buying more stuff because they don't really feel satisfied with what they already have. A purchase that isn't satisfying creates the yearning for another purchase. Round and round it goes. It's comparable to sitting down to a mediocre meal. You feel full, but you don't feel satisfied. You may start eating more to calm your craving even when you aren't hungry. In this way, the cycle of consumption continues.

The things you purchase and don't really want sap your energy. They generate clutter in your surroundings and in your mind. Clutter drags down your creativity. It keeps you stuck where you are. Next time you go shopping, think about whether the item you are contemplating buying will make your life happier, easier, or more fun. *Then* look at the price to determine if you have the money for the purchase. The process goes in that order. How can you know if you like something if you begin by focusing on how much it costs?

Your Desires Are Unique to You

Many women overspend in their efforts to fill a big hole within themselves. Or they spend from habit rather than with conscious intention. As a wise person said, 'You can never have enough of what you don't really want." Remember, your desires are uniquely yours. Nobody is exactly like you. Nobody can tell you what you want. You have the privilege of deciding for yourself. It's your birthright. Keep it sacred. Savor your wants. Value yourself. Honor your truth.

When you are clear about what you want, you are less influenced by advertisements telling you to buy the latest fad. As you look inside yourself and identify your true feelings, you begin to understand what you want, what you feel, what you think, and how you want to live.

As you take control of your life's energy by making conscious choices about what to do and what to buy, you begin to align your goals, dreams, and values with your personal spending decisions. Then you are ready to make purchases consistent with your unique desires. You'll find that when you make very good choices with your money, your money goes further. You get what you want—and you love what you get.

Set Your Intention

When you really know what you want, and you've identified the essence of your desire, you are ready for the next step. That step is to set an intention to have what you want. An intention is not a wish. It is not a hope. It is much stronger than wishes and hopes. Wishing and hoping are weak. Don't hope. Set a firm intention. If you can't set a firm intention about a desire, the chances are good that you really don't want what you say you want. That's okay, too; it just leaves you free to continue figuring out what you really do want. But, sooner or later, you will need to climb into the driver's seat. You must move beyond wishes and hopes if you want to bring in results. You must move to intention.

An intention is a way of connecting your present to your future. You set an intention to bring something into your life that you don't already have. You can use the power of your thoughts, the power of positive thinking, and affirmations to bring your desired future into your present-day reality.

Paradoxes

There's an interesting paradox here. The way intentions and affirmations work is that you affirm you already have what it is you want. You don't say, "It's coming." You say, "It is here now." Does this seem odd? Remember you are working with your unconscious mind, which doesn't know the difference between the things you want and the things you have. If you affirm "It's coming," it will always be on the way. If you affirm "It's here," you will bring it into being. When stating affirmations, choose your words and thoughts very carefully. Little differences do matter.

Let Your Negative Thoughts Move On

Your conscious mind may balk at your affirmations. It may come up with all the reasons and excuses about why you can't have what you want. This is normal. Just let the negative thoughts pass. Of course, just allowing negative thoughts to pass instead of dwelling on them can be a challenging process. The difficulty comes from the fact that negative thoughts are often habitual thoughts, based on fear or lack.

You probably learned these thoughts when you were a child and have never questioned them. You may not even perceive them as negative. When you start to pay attention to your thoughts, you will recognize the negative ones. They will always tell you why you can't have what you want. When a negative thought surfaces, just let it move on. You don't need to stop it or defend yourself or fight it. Just let it pass by. Thinking and feeling are fluid processes. Keep going. Whenever a negative message surfaces, just say "Next . . ." Do not give it any of your precious attention. Throw it away. Next . . . Eventually, you will banish negative thoughts both from your consciousness and your subconscious mind.

When you make an intention to have something you want, you need to be very specific. "My intention is to own a house at the beach within five years." "My intention is to be debt-free within two years." Intentions can be big and small, or daring and mundane. If you set an intention, it will come to pass. This is why it is so important to set specific intentions.

Conscious and Unconscious Intentions

When you set an intention, you are tuning into the laws of the universe. Your thoughts are energy and that energy, transformed by action, creates your desire. You always act according to your conscious and unconscious beliefs. So, if you set an intention and put energy toward it, no matter how little or how much, it will come to pass. It is far better to live your life with conscious intention than with unconscious intention. If you don't live consciously, by default you are living unconsciously. If your conscious mind is continually thinking negative thoughts like, "I can't have what I want," your unconscious mind will create that reality for you, just as you have directed.

If you want to know what your unconscious intentions are, look at the results of your life so far. Everything begins as a belief, a thought, and an intention, either consciously or unconsciously. When you subtract what you consciously created, what you have left is what you unconsciously created. If you are living the life you truly want, then, chances are, you are living with conscious intention. If you aren't, then you are allowing your unconscious mind to create your reality. If you want to give up the struggle, you must align your conscious and unconscious mind so they work together. Begin by exploring your reality versus your desires.

 Think About It . . .

> *Pay attention to your thoughts. Do any of your habitual thoughts sabotage you? Do you find mixed messages that neutralize each other? Are your thoughts and feelings consistent with your behavior? If not, something is out of balance.*

Living with Conscious Intention

Women who live with conscious intention and directed action have many traits in common. Their lives have a sense of ease. They don't seem to worry. They radiate confidence. They seem grounded, not pushed and pulled in one direction after another. They appear content to listen to their hearts and follow their own paths. They aren't swayed by popular culture. Very often, they aren't even in touch with popular culture. They don't buy into the "more is better" belief. They don't care if someone has more than they do. They just live their own lives, making choices consistent with their wishes. They are happy just as they are. Internally focused, they know what they want and they know it is available to them.

Gratitude

Another symptom of living with conscious intention is a strong feeling of gratitude. If you meet someone who exhibits a great deal of humility and gratitude, very likely they are living with conscious intention. They feel good about their lives. They live in a state of grace. They understand they can have anything they want, so they don't feel envious of others. They are just happy to have what they have. They also feel happy when other women get what they want. Good things happen to them. They just go for what they want, without wasting energy on unnecessary distractions. They live their lives to their greatest potential.

Women who live with conscious intention don't spend much energy judging others. Because they are internally focused, they often don't even notice what others have or don't have. They never try to keep up with anybody else. They play the game of life according to their own rules and values. Women who are nonjudgmental also don't need to be "right," or feel any need to impose their feelings on others. They approach life from a solid core because they pay attention to their feelings. They believe what they believe. They feel what they feel. They have no expectations that anyone else should share their beliefs or feelings.

Is It Expensive?

Let's take this idea of living without judgment one step further. Let's look at judgments about money. When somebody asks me if something is expensive, I always reply, "I don't know." This usually elicits an uncomprehending stare and, "How can you not know?" I think the question is really, "How could I know?" Expensive is a judgmental word that means different things to different women. It's the same as talking about "wealth." There are as many definitions of expensive as there are women who think about it.

Two examples come to mind: One day a friend picked me up for lunch in a beautiful, brand new Mercedes. She said, "I got it cheap! Can you believe I only pay $1,000 a month?" To her, $1,000 a month for a car lease is peanuts. To someone else it would be most of their take-home pay. The value of $1,000 is completely relative to how we live and what we think.

The other example comes from a class I taught several years ago. We were talking about wanting and having. One woman said, "I would be happy if I could make $100,000 a year." Another woman promptly responded, "Why do you want to limit yourself like that?" For many women, the thought of earning $100,000 a year stretches the limits of what they think is possible. For the woman who lives without limits and earns $500,000 a year, it isn't enough. It's all in the perspective. Who are we to judge? Both points of view are totally valid to the person who possesses them.

Buy Only What You Truly Want

For many years, if something seemed "too expensive," I told myself I couldn't or shouldn't have it. Sometimes I'd feel guilty for buying something I thought cost too much. Sometimes I wouldn't buy it, even when I had the money. I must have believed I didn't deserve anything so expensive. I don't do that anymore. Now I look at an item and think about the *value* it has for me, not how much it costs. If I have the money and it is exactly what I want, I buy it.

Thirty years ago I bought a pair of salad tongs I was very fond of. I used them until about five years ago when I noticed they didn't look very good anymore. They had tossed one too many salads. I wanted another set. For five years, I looked at salad tongs every time I shopped. I saw lots of salad tongs, but I didn't see any I really liked. Nowadays, I am very clear that I don't buy anything unless I love it and really want it.

Then one day I was in a wonderful craft store on Salt Spring Island in Canada where I saw a pair of salad tongs that nearly made my heart stop. The tongs are forged from pewter. The handles are beautiful hand-polished wood in subdued colors of purple, maroon, and light orange. They are a work of art. I fell in love and bought them. They cost $200. My friends were horrified to learn that I had spent $200 on salad tongs. They judged that to be expensive. They believed they could not afford $200 for a pair of salad tongs.

I believe women don't have the money to buy the things they really want because they buy lots of things they don't really want. I had the money for the salad tongs because I was unwilling to pay even $40 for a pair of salad tongs I didn't really like. I spent five years looking for the perfect salad tongs. Obviously, it wasn't a high priority. I just had it in the back of my mind. I had lots of pleasure looking for, and then finding, the perfect pair. The salad tongs are a source of constant pleasure. I keep them in a drawer with my dish-towels, so even when I'm not using them I see them. I will have them for the rest of my life. Is $200 too much to pay? Is it expensive? I don't know. Is it?

Keeping Up Appearances

Another characteristic of living with intention is having little or no need to have others think well of you. In other words, "What you think of me is none of my business." There is no substitute for looking inside yourself for approval. It is up to you to decide how you want to live. You can't expect to be happy if you give others power over you.

Living for the approval of others can be very damaging. Women who live primarily for others often give up large pieces of themselves in the process. They may become so separated from themselves that they lose their ability to know what they want. It's as if they lose their connection to their own selves. A woman's spirit can get lost in the struggle to maintain appearances. She may get lost in the daily grind of playing her various roles—wife, mother, daughter, worker. I think many women yearn to live more authentically, but are afraid of what might happen if they do. They keep pretending they are fulfilled just to keep the peace.

It can be hard to stop pretending when you've built your life as one who exists for others. It becomes second-nature to internalize other people's expectations of you. You end up sharing those expectations, too. If you meet with rejection or criticism, you believe it. You can't keep up appearances all of the time. Sometimes, the small voice of your authentic self cries to be heard. Listening to it can be risky. But listen you must.

$ Think About It . . .

Now, get your journal and think about the following questions. Then answer them as completely as you can.

- *Are you free to express yourself? Do you allow yourself to do so? What would be the consequences if you stopped pretending? How would your life change if you chose to live more authentically?*

- *Who supports you in being authentic, and who just wants you to look good and play nice? Will the people in your life support you as you try to change?*

* *Do you compare yourself to other women and come up short? Can you stop judging and comparing yourself to others? How would you feel if you did stop judging and comparing yourself to others?*

Detachment: The Challenge

When you know the essence of what you want and you have set a firm intention, it is time to take the third step. You must give up any attachment to the outcome of all of your directed effort and affirmations. This is often the most difficult part. You know what you want, yet you can't be attached to how you will get it. You just need to trust that it's coming.

You might respond to this by saying, "How could I do that? After all the work I had to do just to figure out what I want!" But, strange as it seems, this is the next step. Figure out what you want, set your intention, and then just let it go. Forget about it. You placed your order. You don't need to repeat yourself. Let the universe do its work. You set a conscious intention into motion. Now let the mysterious working of your unconscious mind and the universe do the rest. Your energy unites with the universal energy and your deepest desire will manifest. Or something better. For the highest good of all.

Something Better

These last two points are worth noting. You must understand that your desire may be met with something you never imagined. You must leave room for "this or something better." Of course, you know "better" is a purely subjective term: meaning better for you. A better fit. Your perfect way to experience whatever it is you are to experience. And the phrase "for the highest good of all" is a way to acknowledge we are part of the vast, interconnected universe. We may want what we individually want. But we also need to align with the whole system. We participate in a system so large we can't even comprehend or really understand it. But we have a sense of it. We know it works. And we know selfishness doesn't seem to fit. Allow yourself to win, and others to win, too.

Letting Go of Attachment

Letting go of attachment to a specific outcome allows grace to enter. It's a "release and receive" paradox. For example, I have a friend who wanted to find her perfect mate. Fortunately for her, she remained connected with her intention—a perfect mate—and she let go of everything other than that intention. Because she had let go, she was able to recognize tall, dark, and handsome in a man who is short, bald, and for her, completely adorable. They are blissfully happy together. Good thing she wasn't stuck on the details. Remember, you want to find the *essence* of your desire. Let the universe handle the rest. When viewed from different perspectives, there are many potential answers. Allow the larger picture to support you. The Higher Power (or whatever you call the larger forces in the universe) is very good at connecting the dots.

Taking Action: The Place to Begin

When you have determined the essence of your desire, you have set an intention, and you have let go of attachment to the outcome, you are ready for the final step. This has to do with where you put your attention in the present time. You will not get what you desire without action. As the Bible says, "Faith without works is dead." New Age prophets say, "Head, heart, hands." My personal favorite is, "Vision without action is hallucination." You must align yourself, and act. You can act only in the present. Not the past. Not the future. Right now. Your actions today determine your life today—and tomorrow. As you know, your conscious and unconscious thoughts and beliefs form the foundation from which all of your actions arise. You need to stay aware of all of your thoughts. And you need to take action.

For example, if you set an intention to find the job of your dreams, you need to match your behavior to your intention. You have to look for that job as though looking was a full-time job in itself. You need to write a résumé, talk to people, go on informational interviews, go to agencies, and read the want ads. If you are to get the job of your dreams, you must act as though you already have it. You search as thoroughly and diligently as you can to find it and you don't skimp on the details.

Similarly, if your wish is to get out of debt, you must quit using credit cards, write a spending plan, and live within your means. If your wish is for a clean house, you must pick up a broom. If your desire is for a relationship, you must get out of your house and put yourself in situations where you can meet people.

Time Management

This step is about how you use your time. I live by this axiom, "What I do today is very important because I am exchanging a day of my life for it." Believing this has changed my life because I have paid very close attention to how I use my time. If you use your time in pursuit of your dreams, you will live your dreams. If you use your time in pursuit of someone else's dreams, you will live that person's dreams. If you spend time on activities that don't support your intention, you not only waste your time, you waste your precious life energy. Watch how you use time. Spending time is like spending money. Are you getting good value or are you throwing it away?

Managing your time and taking action are critical for achieving your dreams. If you throw your time away, you are throwing your dreams away as well. This is as true for the mundane, everyday goals of cleaning a garage or washing the dog as it is for loftier goals. If you don't spend time in pursuit of your dreams, you are unlikely to achieve your dreams very soon.

Time is your ally or your obstacle depending upon how you use it. Plan your time so you don't fritter it away. It is precious. On the other hand, be sure to include leisure activities, solitude, and frivolous pursuits in managing your time. Your action plan isn't only about work. It is also about play. If you know you want to lie around the house and read a book all weekend, include it in your action plan. It isn't difficult to balance your time with activities that support you in your fullness when you are aware of your dreams and goals and use your time to fulfill them. When you pay attention to time, your life magically supports you.

 Think About It . . .

Now, get your journal and answer these questions.

- *What do I love to do? What gives me great satisfaction? What am I very good at doing? What do I feel passionate about? When does time stand still? If money were no object, how would I spend my time? When have I felt totally successful and joyful? What was I doing?*

- *Think and write about your ideal day. How would you spend a precious twenty-four hours if you could choose every moment? Who is there? Describe how you feel and why. Can you live your ideal day today? If the answer is no, why?*

CHAPTER FIVE

YOU ALWAYS HAVE A CHOICE

The strongest principle of growth lies in human choice.
George Eliot (1819–1880)

You don't need a crystal ball or a psychic to tell your future. Just examine the choices you make every day. You create your life with your choices. You build your life, financial and otherwise, choice by choice. You literally create your life with your day-to-day choices. As described in earlier chapters, your choices stem from your core beliefs about the world around you. You create, consciously or unconsciously, all the time. You always have choices.

Own Your Choices

If you find yourself in a situation that you initiated, clearly you made a choice to be there. If you find yourself in situation you didn't initiate, you may not have a choice about being in your circumstances, but you can decide how you want to respond. You are never helpless because you have the ability to make choices that support you and what you want, regardless of your circumstances.

You may think of yourself as a victim or something very close to it. *Challenge that belief.* If you believe you are a victim and not in control then, by default, you allow something or someone else to make choices for you. You make the choice to turn over your choice to another. When you do this, you choose to be subject to that other person's wishes and values. By acquiescing, you choose. I think it's very empowering to be responsible and to own all of your choices. And it's powerful to remember that you always have new choices to make, every moment.

Suffering Is Optional

The notion that suffering is optional may be hard to believe, but it's a true statement. We have the opportunity to be a victim or to take responsibility for our choices. I advocate owning choices. If you are suffering, it is because you have made the unconscious choice to suffer. You can make another choice. You can make a choice to own your life and create it the way you want it.

You live with the choices you make every moment. If you are an adult, certainly you can choose where you live, the people with whom you associate and spend your time, and the people to whom you give your love. The only choice that cannot be undone is the choice to have children. Any other choice can be modified or drastically changed.

Sometimes making a choice can be just too difficult. Clearly, you can't know the outcome of your choice until you make it. The anxiety of not knowing may cause you to freeze and you may not want to make a choice at all. However, not choosing is a choice in itself; but it is a weak choice, made from fear rather than strength. When you make a choice with a conscious intention consistent with your goals, dreams, and values, you can trust that your choice will be the best choice.

Of course, there are consequences associated with choices. You may perceive them as losses. But, very often, you have to give up something to get something. You may think of loss as a totally negative concept. Sometimes it is, but often it isn't. For example, when you choose to cut your losses, you are living creatively and powerfully. There is a fine balance in giving up something to get something.

Choose What You Want

When you are given a choice, the first question to ask yourself is, "What do I really want?" The answer that rises up from deep within is the right choice. My friend Alex was recently talking to me about the trouble he was having in relating to his adult children. Alex's wife died not long ago. When she was alive, Alex had made the choice to let her take responsibility for his relationship with his children. She had been his buffer. He didn't really know his kids at all. Now his buffer was gone and if he was going to have a good relationship with his children, it was up to him.

Alex wanted a close relationship with his kids, but he didn't know where to begin. His habit was to throw money at them so they would stay close by. This created a problem. His children related to him only as a source of money. He felt resentful that they didn't seem to care about him. He thought they cared only about his money. So, he attached a lot of strings to the money. He didn't give freely. He tried to control them with his money. This created a situation exactly the opposite of what he wanted. He resented his children and they resented him.

He related his painful experiences with his children to me at length and ended up saying, with his head in his hands, "I don't know what to do." I asked him, "What exactly do you want from your children?" With a flash of anger in his eyes he responded, "What do you mean what do I want? What difference does that make? There's nothing I can do about it."

We debated his point of view for some time before he calmed down. He wanted the only thing we all want in life and that is connection with others. He felt disconnected and used. His children felt disconnected and abused. I suggested that he talk with his children one-on-one and begin to build relationships with them. It could take years to develop the relationships he wants. But the choice to make a conscious effort to get to know his children and to tell them the truth about his feelings is the only place he can start. He knows it will take extraordinary effort, but the positive effects on his life will be worth it.

Today, Alex is slowly building trust by changing his mind about the way he relates to his children. He is trying to give up his attachment to telling them what to do in exchange for money. It's a process that frightens him. For the first time in his life he feels vulnerable to his children. However, he also feels optimistic about the future, even though he still feels angry and resentful that he is in this position. He is often disappointed, yet he is happy he has decided to reach out. He knows he is doing what he can to change the family dynamic. He also knows it is all he can do. He can't change his children. He can only change himself.

Living with Choices Can Be Scary

It is frightening to make choices—especially choices we have never made before. Proactive choices, the ones we initiate, can be especially scary. We don't always know what we're doing. Often it requires a leap of faith. Yet we're still responsible. Implied in any choice is responsibility for the consequences of that choice. Sometimes it is too difficult to know what to do, so we simply do not choose. We let life and circumstances choose for us. Then we can choose to react in any number of ways. But notice, it's still a choice.

Sometimes we agonize over our choices. The conflict is genuine. We want to make the "right" decision, but we can't always see what that might be. I often meet women at just this point in their lives. My clients often come to me when forced to make life choices. I always tell them that when it comes to making life choices, the only "right" decision comes from the heart, not the head.

I believe when we are conflicted over making a choice it is because our thinking is not in alignment with our heart or our true feelings. Our alternatives go around and around in our brain. The feeling interferes with our ability to think. But we continue to believe that we can "think it through." We look to friends and family to help us. The more time goes by, the more anxious we become. We are in a state of total confusion and despair. We know we need to make a choice. Yet we don't or won't. If we stall long enough, the choice to make the choice is gone and we must then live with the consequences of our inaction.

The Marriage Indecision

Suppose you think you should marry the man you are engaged to, but your heart isn't in it. You justify the marriage in numerous ways: "He can provide for me." "I like his family." "He loves me." "I've promised him I will marry him." A thousand reasons for the marriage roll around in your mind. But when you quiet down, feel your body, and listen to your heart, you know in a very visceral way that he is not a good partner for you.

A number of women have reported this kind of stress prior to their marriage. They heard a small voice within themselves repeatedly telling them they were making a mistake, but they chose not to listen. The consequences of calling off a wedding seemed too enormous. "I couldn't disappoint my family and friends." "I would look foolish." "I may never have another chance to get married . . . How bad could it be?"

Their choices have had far-reaching consequences, financial and otherwise. Many of these women spent most of their lives with men they never really loved. In many instances, they made a good life. But deep down, they know they would make a different choice given the chance to do it over.

Some women are stuck in a job, a marriage, or a dance of anger with a parent. They don't see any way out. They don't see the choices they made that took them where they are. Now they don't see they have a choice about how to get somewhere else. They are stuck in the illusion that someone else controls their lives. They are afraid to be in charge of their own lives. I like this quote from Marianne Williamson (1992): "Our deepest fear is not that we are inadequate. Our deepest fear is that we are powerful beyond measure."

Think About It . . .

Now, take out your journal and after thinking about it for a while, describe a time when you were faced with a choice that you didn't want to make.

- *What were the circumstances?*

- *How did you feel as you made the choice? Did you review all of your options or did you look at one single choice?*

- *Did you enlist the insight of your friends and family or did you feel too threatened to share your need to choose?*

- *What was the outcome of your choice? Is your life better because of your choice?*

- *Knowing what you know now, could you have made a better choice?*

Tell somebody about what you have learned about yourself and the choices you have made that have created your circumstances.

You can also think and write about a seemingly innocent choice that changed your life forever. Maybe you decided to go to college in one place instead of another and you met your life partner. Maybe you decided to put off having children until it was too late. Or perhaps you met someone casually and then landed the job of your dreams. You learn about yourself when you review your life choices, see the forks in the road, and weigh the consequences of having made one choice over another.

In the future, when you must make a difficult choice, make a written list of the circumstances and the various alternatives open to you. Writing it all down helps you to be more objective. The right choice will appear as you write and process. It comes up from your body as a feeling and then a thought or an answer begins to emerge. Quiet your mind, so you can listen to your heart.

Fear of Truth

Many choices are made unconsciously, from a place of fear. For example, if we are afraid we might be in trouble with creditors, we may ignore their letters or telephone calls. Deep down, we know they aren't going to go away. But we choose to ignore the issue until dealing with it becomes unavoidable, and at that point, the problem is often much bigger than it was in the beginning. Our choice to ignore problems instead of facing them head on creates new problems in two ways:

1. The problem gets bigger the longer we ignore it.

2. We live in a constant state of anxiety until we face the situation squarely.

The anxiety is often the bigger issue. We intuitively know when something needs to be dealt with. By choosing to ignore it, we usually end up living with a high level of anxiety and perhaps fear. Then the fear turns to anger, and the anger eventually is directed toward the self. We can avoid this cycle by acting responsibly at the onset of a crisis or challenge.

Stay in Control

Many people believe they are powerless to take control over their own money. But there is never a time when you are not in control of your money. You can choose to exercise that control or not. Consider Andy who owed the IRS several years of back taxes. He said they had demanded payment of $600 a month. But he did not have $600 to send them every month. He knew that he could send them $350 and still stay current with his living expenses. I suggested he call the IRS and tell them that payments of $350 a month would be the best he could do. When he heard that his eyes got big, even teared up a little. He said, "I can't tell the IRS how much I can pay them. They won't listen to me."

As we discussed the issue further, Andy became quite emotional. He was scared to death of the IRS. He also felt a great deal of shame about his situation. He told me he was always very apologetic when he talked with them. To avoid feeling humiliated by them, he was willing to agree to pay $600 a month even though he knew he didn't have the money. He said he would rather die than negotiate a payment plan.

I suggested he had a choice about how to approach the situation with the IRS. He could choose to negotiate from a position of strength. He could, for example, not apologize at all. He could firmly state his commitment to pay them $350 a month, and not mention either the shame he felt or their wish for payments of $600 a month. It had never occurred to him that he had a choice in his negotiations. His fear and shame had stopped him from being able to see beyond fear and shame.

 Think About It . . .

The next time you are in a difficult situation with another person, be silent and don't react until you choose the response that fits your desires. Do not respond from habit. You may not be able to respond right away because you need to know what you want before you can respond appropriately. Negotiate the timeliness of your response and be very clear that you are making a choice to take care of yourself. Observe how powerful you feel when you respond from strength rather than from habit. Notice how the situation changes when you choose your response rather than react emotionally from fear.

Speak Up

Sometimes, particularly where money matters are concerned, we become paralyzed with fear. You may be afraid to tell a friend you don't want to dine at an expensive restaurant. You may be afraid to tell your young child that you don't have the money to pay for dancing lessons or your adult children that you can't help them financially when they need it. When you are afraid to say you don't know how you can pay for college or the wedding, this fear may be compounded because you may also be afraid to look bad in front of others.

You may be afraid to tell others that you are deeply in debt. You are afraid of what they will think. And you are afraid you will lose their love or respect. The irony is this fear couldn't be further from the truth. When you make a choice to take care of yourself, and you share that choice with others, they respond in a loving way. People can tell when you're telling the truth. They know when you speak and act from a place of integrity.

As a role model, you are giving them a gift. When you speak the truth, others are given the opportunity to witness an adult making a life choice that is counter to what they want in the moment. This is what adults do. They take care of themselves. They connect their choices today with their life in the future.

Create in the Moment

You create your life by the little choices you make moment by moment. The big, critical choices take care of themselves through the small choices you make day to day. When you stay centered, your choices are made from desire. When you are not centered, you may defer making a decision or you may default to habit.

Choosing from habit rather than from conscious intention probably creates more havoc in our lives than anything else. When we choose to let our habits guide us, our life has a certain sameness to it. We have the same feelings over and over again. The players may change. The circumstances may be different. But our feelings are the same. As Edna St. Vincent Millay wrote, "It is not true that life is one damn thing after another. It's one damn thing over and over." This is certainly true for people who choose to live on automatic pilot.

Hold Your Power

If you feel safe, the chances are good that you understand you are in charge. If you feel unsafe, you may have transferred your power to someone or something else. When you give your power away, you feel diminished. It's understandable. It's also changeable, simply by changing your mind. There are no circumstances where you are powerless, unless you make the choice to be powerless. Or, as Eleanor Roosevelt put it, "Nobody can make you feel inferior without your consent."

I meet many women who are getting divorced. Jean is fairly typical. She's forty-eight, and she's been married for twenty-five years. Her husband woke up one morning and made the grand announcement. "The marriage is over." Jean was stunned. She felt shock, grief, rage, shame, and a myriad of emotions, as you can well imagine. Now, Jean has no power over her husband. She cannot force him to make a different choice. *We are forever powerless over other people's choices.* He chooses whatever he chooses. Jean does, however, have a great deal of choice as to how she deals with her situation. She can be a victim. Or she can move forward, making choices in her best interest, moment by moment. *We always have ultimate power in choosing how we respond.*

Choice and Medical Decisions

Another area to practice making good choices is in relation to the medical profession, which, of course, also relates to money. Nothing costs more over the long term than poor health. Over the years, I've heard many horror stories from women who misplaced their trust in doctors and learned to regret their choices.

I've heard from several women who delayed treatment of breast cancer because they didn't believe they could question their doctor's opinion. They trusted the doctor when they heard, "It's probably nothing. Let's just watch it." They knew something was wrong, but they didn't want to appear too assertive in an area where they did not feel like an expert.

My sister, Anne, has saved her own life more than once by insisting on her own choice of medical treatment. Several years ago, her oncologist assured her that a tumor in her uterus was benign. The doctor needed to go out of town and suggested that Anne put off the surgery until "after the first of the year." That was in mid-October. Anne said, "No. I've had breast cancer. I've had a melanoma. I want the tumor removed next week. If you can't do it, can you recommend someone else?" She was very polite, but very determined. She was willing to take responsibility for her health and to make a choice consistent with her desires.

Ten days later, the doctor, and our family, were devastated to learn that Anne's tumor was the most virulent form of uterine cancer. But there was also good news. The cancer was totally contained. It had not spread anywhere else in Anne's body. Uterine cancer is a deadly form of cancer because it is so difficult to detect before it has spread. There are no symptoms.

If Anne had made the choice to pay attention to the doctor's best interest rather than her own, she might not be alive today. The tumor had doubled in size from the time of her office appointment to her surgery, ten days later. Anne's choice gave her a much better chance at living. It was literally a life or death decision. And she didn't even know it. Anne just knows she is responsible for herself and her health. She is willing to take care of herself, even when that means going against her doctor's advice.

Your life becomes much easier when you live gracefully with your power to choose. You just take care of yourself the best you can, and make the best choices you can with the information you have at the time. You can be proactive or reactive, as you choose. You are not easily intimidated, because you aren't stuck in any position. You can choose to be flexible. Or you can choose to stand firm. Whatever serves you best. You are willing to be wrong. You are willing to forgive. You are courageous in pursuit of your own dreams. You are loving and accepting because you are creating your own life with purpose, spontaneity, and grace.

Positive Affirmations Help

Sometimes it is difficult to start making conscious choices. Now let's suppose you're clear about your desires. Then you can use affirmations to help you create your life intentionally. Affirmations are a powerful tool to help your unconscious mind loosen up and become unstuck. They are little sayings you attach to your bathroom mirror, the visor of your car, your desk, or near the kitchen sink. Anywhere you look, there they are. They remind you. They help you to re-orient your perspective. They help you to stay awake and focused. They help you to remember what you want.

An affirmation is a phrase that helps you focus on what you want to bring into your life. It is a statement of intention and fact. It is always stated in the present tense, as if it is already a fact. For example, if you want to get out of debt, you could write an affirmation that says, "I am debt-free." Or if you want a new job, your affirmation could state, "I have a job I love that pays me well." (Only you know what "pays me well" means.) You could affirm, "I have a healthy body," or "I have everything I need right now."

There are no limits to the kinds of affirmations you can use. Just be sure they are short and that they truly reflect what you want to bring into your life. Remember, affirmations must always be stated in the present tense ("I am" rather than "I will") and they're always in the positive rather than the negative form ("I am" rather than "I am not").

Affirmations are easy. They are nothing more than declaring that you already have what you desire. This is a very deliberate form of self-talk, and it is very powerful. You create your life with affirmations, consciously or unconsciously. Make the choice to affirm how you want to experience your life, thought by thought. Make conscious choices.

Keep in mind, as stated in chapter 4, an affirmation isn't a hope or a wish. An affirmation is a firm commitment. It is a powerful statement of your intention to have your desire. It is a statement you make to yourself and to the world at large. Stand in the power of your own words.

There are many books that describe the power of affirmations. Years ago, Shakti Gawain (1983) wrote one called *Creative Visualization*. It is a classic. Affirmations may work for you. Give them a try.

Failure: Another Illusion

What happens when you make a choice that doesn't turn out very well? Where you didn't anticipate or like the outcome? You may have the idea that you failed. Perhaps your marriage didn't work out, or your children are in trouble. You feel responsible. For whatever reason, you feel your choice did not measure up to your intention.

When you encounter a disappointment in life, you can either perceive it is as a failure or you can welcome it as a learning experience. There is a life lesson in each one of your challenges. You learn the lessons when you move from perceiving experiences as failure and stopping there (basking in your own judgment), and move into the perception that life has many lessons that we're all learning; and you're a wiser woman after each lesson.

In my life, I have been given the opportunity many times to learn that I cannot control another person. I may not like that my marriage ended, but I have grown in ways that were previously unimaginable to me. I have been able to spend time alone and create a different life that supports my full self-expression.

I'm not sure that it is possible to fail. It is difficult for me to think in terms of failure. As I see it, you set a clear intention, stay in your integrity, make the best choices you can, and give up any attachment to the outcome. The desire is always for "This or something better, for the highest good of all." You might not achieve the result you intended, but it isn't a failure, it is just a different outcome. It might take time to recognize the gift inherent in the unexpected. Very often, the gift we were not expecting is so much bigger than what we could imagine. Look for the gifts in every "failure." You may find some real gems.

The idea that you build your life by the choices you make assumes that you believe you have ultimate control and power over your life experiences. You choose to live consciously or unconsciously every single day. Why not make the choice to live consciously, with clear intention? If you do this, you will live the life you were meant to live. You just have to choose it. You can live your life in peace or chaos. The choice is yours.

CHAPTER SIX

LOVE AND MONEY

Life shrinks or expands in proportion to one's courage.
Anais Nin (1903–1977)

If you are planning to be married, already married, or facing a separation or divorce, this chapter will be of particular interest to you. The subject of money is relevant because marriage, separation, and divorce are legal processes. If you dissolve a committed relationship that does not have the legal status of marriage, the law does not protect you. You and your partner are basically on your own. However, many of these suggestions will work for you, even if you are not legally married. So review the chapter for relevant information.

Cohabitation Agreements

If you plan to live with your partner without being married, have an attorney prepare a cohabitation agreement. You may be reluctant to talk about money before you start living with your partner, but having a financial agreement in advance will strengthen your relationship. A *cohabitation agreement* spells out in detail how you will manage your joint finances. It defines the terms of your living together and the disposition of the assets in the event you separate. It also protects you and your partner from the pain of figuring out how to divide the assets if you separate. It is like having a prenuptial agreement.

Discussing a cohabitation agreement can be helpful because it forces you to talk about money before you live together. If are comfortable discussing money with your partner in this setting, it is very likely that you are both operating on the same wavelength. For the agreement, you both will need to list all of your assets as an exhibit. The two of you will also need to list all of your debts as another exhibit. This is wonderful because it means that neither of you will run into any surprises down the line. This is also true for prenuptial agreements.

Prenuptial Agreements

Prenuptial agreements can be tricky. You may not want considerations about money to intrude into your romantic relationship. This is a common feeling. Nevertheless, if you enter a marriage owning a fair amount of assets, you should consider using a prenuptial agreement to protect them in the event of a divorce. If you decide you want a prenuptial agreement, proceed carefully and cautiously. Give your fiancé time to review it and discuss it with you. Your goals are to prepare for a wonderful life together and to protect your assets at the same time.

If your fiancé asks you to sign a prenuptial agreement, discuss it calmly and thoughtfully with him. Do not interpret his request as a lack of trust or any other kind of negative sign. A prenuptial agreement doesn't mean he won't share his worldly goods with you or treat you well. It just means that he wants to take care of himself. You want to marry someone who takes good care of himself. However, if you feel pressured or under duress to agree to the terms, do not sign such an agreement. Furthermore, such pressure could be a red flag as to the desirability of the marriage. A prenuptial agreement is also important if you both have significant net worth. As with any kind of agreement between loving partners, you want to have direct and honest communication. Listing your assets and debts helps to build trust even before you marry.

Marriage and Money

If you are married, like millions of women your focus is primarily on your responsibilities to home and family. If you work outside the home, you may feel pressed for time and overwhelmed with all there is to do. You may pay the bills and do most of the shopping. But you may not have the time, energy, or interest to become involved in such matters as retirement plans, savings accounts, and investing. You may feel you are better off leaving those kinds of money decisions to your husband. This can be a risky proposition.

Marriage and money are intimately connected. It is critical that you and your husband learn how to talk openly and honestly about money—the earlier in the marriage, the better. Honest communication about money makes honest communication possible in other areas. It's really not optional. Sooner or later, you will face money issues. Your marriage will be stronger if you are brave enough and skilled enough to participate in the family's decisions about money.

If you are married to a man who is not open to discussing money with you, be careful. I would question whether if he has your best interests in mind. If he loves you and views you as an equal, he will want you to participate in the marriage as an equal partner. If he wants you to remain financially in the dark like a child, you may be in for a rough road.

Understanding Your Financial Life

You may believe that your husband is making wise investments because he is bringing home the bigger paycheck. But this may be an illusion. It may or may not be true. Become proactive and educate yourself about your money, individually and jointly.

- Read and understand your tax returns before you sign them. Ask questions of your accountant or tax preparer until you know what the information reveals about your finances.

- Keep track of your insurance yourself. Know what kind of insurance you have and what it will pay if you need to use it.

- Participate in the spending and investing decisions. Know exactly what you spend every month. Learn about your family investments and retirement plans. For example, find out if the investments are in joint names or single names. Retirement plans are always held in one person's name. Other investment portfolios can be held in joint names. Learn about investing and understand your investment alternatives.

Cash of Your Own

Make sure you have access to cash that is readily available to you. Keep a personal checking account or money in a savings account. The amount can vary depending on your financial circumstances and your perceived need. This money is for use in the event of an emergency. Over the years, I have seen many women who were blindsided when their husbands left them without even the means to buy groceries or gas for their car. I've also known many penniless women who had been married to men with millions of dollars in investment and retirement accounts. Yet, these women had no access to cash or credit. They had to borrow money from friends or relatives so they could hire a divorce lawyer and pay the required retainer.

Having money of your own to spend and manage as you see fit makes you feel better in your marriage because it indicates you are in a partnership, not a parent-child relationship. This is good for everyone in the family.

You also need to have access to credit in your own name. If participation in making the family's money decisions is a new idea for you, begin slowly. Don't make a big pronouncement. Just start educating yourself. Take classes at your community college, read books on money management, and read the business section of the newspaper.

 ## Think about it . . .

Decide you want to talk with your husband about money. Plan to have the discussion at a time when you are both feeling calm and peaceful. Ask him how he feels about his retirement plans. Here are some specific questions that you should ask:

- *When does he plan to retire?*

- *Is he putting money away now?*

- *How is it invested?*

Tell him your ideas about retirement and investing. After your meeting, keep up the dialogue. You don't want to create conflict, but you do want to get smart. If you are not working outside the home, talk with him about contributing to a spousal IRA. You can put $2,000 away every year. (Editor's Note: The IRS puts a $2,000 cap on what you can put into an IRA account, but Congress is considering raising the cap.

Try to reach agreements about how you are going to spend and invest your money. Once your husband realizes you are serious, he may warm up to the idea of including you in the money decisions. In the final analysis, you are responsible for yourself. Your husband is not responsible for you. It is up to you to know how you are going to live now and in the future.

Flying Solo

The legal process for divorce varies from state to state. Research the divorce laws in your state so you will know what to expect. Here are some broad guidelines for separating the money from the marriage. The more you know, the better prepared you will be. Divorce may be the most important financial transaction you will ever make. Yet, you may be in a very vulnerable position. This is particularly true if you have not paid very much attention to money. The more you understand the family finances, the better off you are in the marriage and in the event of separation or divorce. If you have not paid attention to money before, you now have a great opportunity to get involved.

This advice holds true even when there is not very much money to divide. If you have more debts than assets, you may not relate to the information in this chapter. Still, I encourage you to pay attention because the suggestions are based on solid financial concepts. They are valid concepts regardless of your circumstances. Read through the chapter with the understanding that you want to make different choices in the future than you have in the past. You want to build your net worth over time so you won't find yourself in this situation again.

Always remember it is your money too. Your husband may have earned the money while you were taking care of your home, but the money and property you are dividing in your divorce settlement is as much yours as it is your husband's. You have both the right and the obligation to take what is legally and morally yours. Don't fall into the trap of believing that because your husband earned the money, it is more his than yours. This just isn't true.

It is probably true, though, that the person who earned the income wants to keep it. If this isn't you, you must understand that you made your contribution to the family welfare and you deserve equitable treatment. If you go through your property settlement discussions with feelings of unworthiness, you are not likely to make very good financial decisions. The legal system does not care how you feel. You need to take care of yourself.

The Impact of Divorce on Women and Children

The most well-known statistic regarding the devastating financial impact of divorce on women and children was found in a 1985 study by Lenore Weitzman of Harvard University. It states that a woman's standard of living declines 73 percent after a divorce, while a man's *climbs* by 42 percent (Medved 1989).

I have seen numerous rebuttals to these figures but none to Weitzman's main findings that at all income levels, after a divorce, women are much poorer than men and that the wives and children of well-to-do families suffer the greatest relative deprivation. Furthermore, according to 1993 figures, the poverty rate for children living with divorced mothers was 38 percent compared with 11 percent for children raised in two-parent families (Zill and Winquist-Nord 1994).

A Carnegie Corporation report (1994) states that 9 percent of children in the total population who are younger than fifteen live on welfare. The number doubles to 18 percent in the first four months after their parents' separation. The younger the child, the higher the poverty level. Fifty-five percent of children younger than six whose parents had been divorced or separated live below the poverty level. Of course, in recent years, these figures changed and will continue to change, but Weizman's main finding that divorce has a much heavier financial impact on women and children than on men continues to be true. The Carnegie study also found that 50 percent of the total population of children younger than age eighteen will experience their parents divorcing.

The economics of divorce actually have gotten worse over the past fifty years. During the 1950s or 1960s when a couple divorced, the woman usually did not work outside the home. This scenario changed in the 1970s. Today, it is a commonplace that in the majority of marriages, both partners work. In 1998, in 61 percent of married-couple families, both husband and wife worked outside the home. Only 13 percent of families fit the traditional model with the wife as homemaker and the husband as wage earner (Bureau of Labor Statistics 1999).

This brings up an interesting point. If both parties work outside the home, then there is no new opportunity for the couple to bring in more income after the divorce. They are already doing what they can. When a traditional marriage breaks up, the opportunity is there to bring in another income. Very often it is the wife who has not been working. She can get a job. However, it's no cakewalk. She may find it difficult to suddenly support herself especially if she is older and has been out of the labor force for a number of years.

Managing Your Emotions During Divorce

Divorce stirs up profound feelings of grief, anger, and fear. Managing your emotions can feel like a full-time job. If you are in the process of divorce, I suggest you indulge yourself with extraordinary self-care techniques. Make time to take long baths, light candles, breathe deeply, and practice relaxation techniques. Watch out for negative self-talk. You experience your life according to your thoughts, so try to remain positive even in the face of apparent catastrophe. Try to paint a positive picture of your husband. Turning him into an enemy does not support your personal growth. Focus your attention on yourself and on your life going forward.

Stay positive when discussing possible property settlement alternatives with your financial advisors and friends. Try to keep an open mind about what your husband will or won't do. Clients often say to me, "My husband will never agree to that." I try to challenge their negative thinking. More often than not, we come up with a rational, reasonable plan and the husband does agree. Sometimes, men do more than their minimum legal obligation. Give your husband a chance to be generous. He just might surprise you. The more positive you can be during your divorce transition, the smoother it will go. You may reach a better settlement if you remain true to yourself and know unequivocally what it is you want. Focusing on the finances of the divorce can help you move through the experience more gracefully.

Care of the Children

Children experience profound grief and loss when their parents divorce. The best thing you can do for your children is to stay focused, move forward, and be as supportive of their father as possible. The best divorces leave both parties as whole as possible. The object is to take care of yourself and your children, not to get even with your husband. Support your children throughout the entire process. Talk to them about how their lives are going to change. Assure them you and their father will continue to love them and will still take care of them. Realize you are divorcing their father, they aren't. Expect them to love you both and make every effort to protect them from experiencing the marital discord.

Separate the Emotional Trauma from the Money

Divorce can be traumatic to everyone concerned; you, your husband, your children, your family, and friends. I have observed, however, that many women fail to focus on the money issues when divorcing. They feel vulnerable about the uncertainty of their future and they continue to focus on the loss of the relationship. You will be more successful in your divorce, both emotionally and financially, if you can separate the two issues. This takes courage and constant positive self-talk.

Talk to professionals about the financial considerations of your divorce rather than discussing these matters with your family and friends. Well-intentioned friends may not have the knowledge, experience, and perspective to help you make the best choices. Financial planners, lawyers, and CPAs are skilled and experienced at helping people make this difficult transition. Use professionals. They're worth it.

The Challenges of Divorce

Divorce is a time to put away your assumptions and think creatively. Many women sabotage their financial futures by believing their life will go on as usual after a divorce. It is understandable that you might not want to your life to change. You may want to stay in your house. and to keep your children in the same school. This is understandable, but keep an open mind. Selling your house, for example, may be a good idea or it may not. In any case, it is extremely unrealistic to believe that two families can maintain the same lifestyle as one, particularly if there is only one income.

Change is difficult, but if you are getting divorced, you have no choice but to change. Your marriage is over. Change has already taken place. You are now free to build your new life as you want it to be, choice by choice. Your choice to take responsibility for your divorce is very important to your future. This is true for your emotional stability, as well as for your future financial well-being.

As a rule, the law looks at the length of the marriage when determining some of the property settlement issues. A long-term marriage is usually considered one that has lasted longer than twenty-five years. An intermediate-term marriage is usually defined as lasting between ten and twenty-five years. A short-term marriage is one of less than ten years in duration.

The Long-Term Marriage

If you are ending a long-term marriage, you may want to work with a professional who can help you reinvent yourself and build a new, more self-affirming identity. I think this can be one of the most exciting opportunities that life offers a woman. You can move through the most painful divorce and emerge into a new, wonderful, fulfilling life. Now you can take the opportunity to express yourself and live according to your own wishes. For older women who do not have children at home this time can be a golden opportunity.

If you are divorcing after an intermediate- or a short-term marriage, the property settlement discussion usually takes on a different tone. The law isn't as supportive as it is for long-term marriages. Usually, in these instances, you are younger and more capable of supporting yourself. If you are older, you may or may not have supported yourself sometime in the past. The courts take these factors into consideration.

Your Relationship with Your Former Husband

If you have children, you must realize you will remain in some form of relationship with your husband for a long time, even though you are getting divorced. Even if you do not have children, you may seriously want to stay friends with your soon-to-be former husband. But friendship is a two-way street. First determine whether your husband is interested in maintaining a friendship with you. If he isn't interested, you will need to adjust. He may change over time, but don't count on it. Your life will go on and so will his. If you exchange assets for a friendship that likely won't exist after the divorce, you are making a big mistake.

Don't give up something you want during the property settlement because you don't want to anger your husband. True friendship can't be bought. It is great to remain friendly, but it may be unrealistic to believe you will be friends. Of course, your divorce is different than anyone else's. Just be careful when you are making your choices. Make choices that will support you and your new life. Don't make choices that will support your husband in his new life. Of course, it's best if you can do both. But, don't choose his needs over your own.

The Preplanning Process

Planning your divorce will reduce the time and energy you spend. It may reduce your attorney's fees as well. Proper planning will help you to stay focused when your emotions threaten to overwhelm you. As soon as you believe you may be headed for a divorce, go over the family finances with a financial professional.

Preplanning: Steps to Success

1. Gather together all of your financial information. You may need to see a financial advisor who can tell you what you need to know and how to get the information. This is a good thing to do even if you are not under the threat of divorce. All women need to know the details of their family's finances. But if you expect to go through a separation or divorce, you need to know this information now.

2. Suspend judgment about your finances. Look at the money as unemotionally as possible. There is what there is. You can't change things now. But you can decide how to proceed with the rest of your life. If there isn't enough money, you can set an intention to create more money from now on.

3. Make sure you have credit in your own name. If you and your husband have joint credit cards, get a credit card in your own name as soon as you have an inkling that divorce might be on the horizon. You don't want to merely be an authorized user of his card. Note that it may be more difficult for you to establish credit in your own name if you have not worked outside the home. Creditors generally do not count support payments as income unless you have been receiving them regularly in the past, which is usually not the case.

    If you have joint credit cards or a carry a mortgage with both you and your husband's names on it, you are responsible for that debt no matter what your divorce decree states. Your creditor is not a party to your divorce and is not bound by its terms. If your ex-husband doesn't make the payments, your creditors will look to you.

4. Determine what your financial needs will be in the future. Write a detailed list of all of your expenses. Figure out what it will cost you to live each month. Take the time to gather all the information you will need. Don't guess. Don't make estimates. Try to come up with realistic and exact numbers. As you review your spending, recognize that your life is changing. Do not assume you need to keep your house. Don't even assume you need to live in a house. Everything is up for

grabs. Do not cling to the life you had.

Let go of what you spend out of habit and determine what is really important to you. Even with a tight budget, find something you truly want, such as a reliable car or a weekly manicure and include it in your monthly spending plan. Eliminate items that are just habits and are not essential to your feeling of well-being.

Be sure to figure out your expenses month by month. An annual accounting isn't as helpful as a monthly accounting. Convert annual figures to monthly costs. For example, if you pay your car insurance twice a year, add the two payments together and divide by twelve to get the monthly amount. Refine this list over and over again until you know exactly what you need every month, even if you don't pay monthly bills for some items. (See chapter 7.)

5. Consider the tax consequences. A divorce will probably bring up a variety of tax issues. For example, you must pay taxes on any spousal support you receive. Conversely, you can deduct spousal support if you pay it. You don't pay taxes on child support. You will both need to decide who gets to take the children as tax deductions. There are many other tax details that will need to be settled. Talk to a CPA before you sign anything.

6. List all the assets you and your husband have accumulated during your marriage. Include everything—real estate, checking and savings accounts, retirement plans in each of your names, financial investments outside of your retirement assets. Add all of the assets together so you will know exactly what you have to divide.

7. Next, examine any debt obligations. Write down the balances on credit cards, student loans, second mortgages, and credit lines. Include everything, including personal loans. Add them up and subtract them from your assets.

8. Subtract your debt from your assets to determine your net worth. This is a very important figure. The higher your net worth, the better. If you have a negative net worth, meaning you owe more than you own, you will have to get going to improve your financial situation. I've talked with women who didn't know they had a negative net worth until they got divorced. They were horrified to discover they had been living on credit most of their married lives. As I've said

previously, you do yourself a favor when you go through this process, even if you are in a healthy, happy marriage.

9. The final part of the preplanning process is to know "to the penny" your total family income. Review all of your sources of income from pay stubs to inheritances. When you have a clear idea of your gross income, subtract your tax obligations, federal, state, and local taxes, from your total gross income to arrive at your net income.

If your home needs repairs or you want to go back to school, note these items on a separate paper. This list is like a pent-up demand list (see chapter 4). You want to know what your expenses are going to be as a single person. If you need clothes to go to work, note that. If you need a car, write it down. Knowing what your expenses will be for the next several years will help you understand your financial situation even better. You won't be devastated by a sudden big expense. Your net worth and your income are the sources of money you have to work with in negotiating your divorce agreement. When you know what you need and what there is to work with, you are ready to discuss a property settlement agreement. You are not ready until you have this information.

Property Settlement Issues

I believe the single most important asset in any marriage is the ability to earn an income. This frequently walks out the door with the husband. (Sadly, it is still true that women earn less than men do.) I encourage you to factor your income-earning prospects into the property settlement in some way. If you earn less than your husband does, try to get more of the assets. For example, perhaps you can receive more than fifty percent of the retirement money, or you might ask for more of the equity in the house.

The retirement funds are the second most important assets in the marriage because they continue to grow tax-deferred until retirement. Retirement benefits are based on income, so if your husband earns more than you do, he probably has more in his in retirement plan than you do. In such cases, fair doesn't have to mean equal. If your husband has a much larger income than you do, and you get 75 percent of his 401(k) plan, that seems fair to me. If you have no salary or a much lower salary, you may never be able to put away as much as he can. There are many women who are poor in their old age because they divorced and split the retirement assets right down the middle. Their husbands retire comfortably because they were able to continue to add to their retirement funds. The settlement may look equal, but it sure isn't fair.

Don't exchange retirement assets for something else such as your house. You may want to keep your house, but it may not be the best idea in the long run. Maintaining your house costs you money and it isn't liquid. Well-invested retirement assets will grow over time. Stay flexible and be willing to make sacrifices in the present so that you can achieve financial security in the future.

Include cars and personal property, such as artwork, jewelry, and tools only if they are of extraordinary value. I suggest separating your personal property from the property settlement agreement. As a rule, it makes sense for each person to have his or her own car. It's good if you can own your car debt-free. If your husband has a valuable gun collection, the chances are good that you don't want it anyway. The value can be transferred to something you do want. The idea is to remain reasonable about dividing "the stuff." Usually, it's not worth fighting for. Focus on the long term. You can buy another dining set or a bed. When you approach life from a position of strength, you will create everything you want or need anyway.

Planning a divorce isn't difficult, but it may take a bit of sleuthing to get all the facts and figures. The more complicated your family finances, the more difficult it will be. You may need a financial professional to help you sort things out. If the family finances are simple and straightforward, you can do them yourself. It is a good idea, though, to discuss your findings with a professional to be sure you aren't overlooking anything.

Plan for the Present and for the Future

It is natural to focus on the present to the exclusion of the future. But this is a mistake. The present is important, but you must pay attention to what you will need in the future. Children grow up. It is very likely that you will need more money to care for them as they get older. Think about the costs of after-school activities, orthodontics, summer camps, sports involvement, and college expenses. Perhaps your children will need professional counseling for a time. Factor these expenses into your property settlement agreement. You may not name them item by item, but you must have a clear understanding of who is responsible for paying for which items. Determine who is responsible for your children's out-of-pocket medical bills and health insurance premiums. These are very important and are often overlooked. Think about the details and spell things out in the agreement. This will help everyone. The children will know who is going to pay for their college educations and so will you. Clarifying these agreements now can save court costs and hurt feelings in the future.

The Divorce Team

You may benefit by hiring a good therapist, supportive and knowledgeable financial advisors, and an attorney whose expertise is in family law. If these people work as a team, it will help you to stay focused and on track. Each member of your team plays an important part. The court exists to uphold the law, not to make sure you get a fair settlement. The court assures a fair trial. The attorney knows the law and is expert at writing the legal documents. Your financial advisor will help you determine what you need and how to make the most of the marital assets. A CPA will assess the tax impact of your choices.

Your Attorney

Your knowledge of the divorce laws in your state will help you talk to your advisors. It will also help you understand your options. The better educated you are, the better you will feel and the more likely you will be to reach an appropriate agreement. Be sure to retain a family law attorney. Neither your corporate lawyer nor your real estate lawyer is a good choice, even if they charge less money. Working with lawyers who specialize in divorce is important for the following reasons:

1. Family lawyers know the law and can help you understand your legal rights.

2. They can help you with the legal issues affecting your children.

3. They are skilled at structuring property settlement agreements so that ambiguities are eliminated. This is very important.

You are more likely to reach a good compromise when both you and your husband have competent, well-respected family lawyers representing you. The lawyers who practice family law in your area are likely to know each other and they understand how to negotiate with each other.

Working with Your Attorney

1. Determine how well you and your spouse can work together. The more cooperation you can foster, the less you will have to involve attorneys and the less money you will spend.

2. Choose a lawyer who makes you feel comfortable. Do you want someone who tends toward mediation or toward litigation, or do you want someone who will play it somewhere in between? Litigation costs more. You might choose someone whose style contrasts with yours. For example, if you tend to be acquiescent, you might want to choose someone who is more adversarial.

3. Determine whether you can settle without a big battle or if you are more likely to go to trial. If you go to trial, you need to put aside more money. You will also have to brace yourself for an emotionally wrenching experience. If you have never been to court before, this may be an intimidating experience.

4. Understand your attorney's billing rates, procedures, and estimated total cost. Who is paying the bill? You or your husband. It is very likely you will have to give your lawyer a retainer before she agrees to represent you.

5. Make the most of your time with your attorney. Know what you want to discuss and have all of the information in hand before you go to the attorney's office for an appointment and before you initiate a telephone conference. Remember, you pay for every minute you are in conversation with the attorney. Stick to the facts during your conversations.

6. Do not use your lawyer as your therapist.

7. Do what your lawyer tells you to do. You are paying for advice. You are better off to take it. If your lawyer's advice doesn't make sense to you, talk it over until you reach a mutual understanding and agreement. One of you may be lacking an important piece of information. Or you may need a different lawyer. But check it our first.

8. Be honest with your lawyer. If you are having an affair, tell her. She can't help you if she doesn't know all of the facts. She isn't there to judge you. She wants to help you get what you want and need.

9. Don't let your lawyer intimidate you. If you are uncomfortable with your lawyer, find someone else. You don't need to agree on everything, but you do need trust and a good working relationship.

10. Find a lawyer who is reliable and who keeps her commitments. Tell your lawyer what you expect and hold her accountable. For example, you expect her to keep your appointments and to return your telephone calls promptly, you expect your documents to be ready when they are promised, and you expect to receive regular updates on the progress of your case.

Your Financial Advisors

Your financial advisors will help you to wade through the paper work and make sense of your financial picture. You can work with a financial planner or someone who specializes in finance and money management. This person can work with your accountant to ensure that all of the tax implications to your settlement are addressed. Your financial advisor can assist you in structuring a settlement proposal that you can give to your attorney. In this capacity, financial advisors often work with lawyers. They understand what you need, what you have, and how various settlement alternatives would play out. Your divorce planning will pay off when you enter the settlement process. You will be armed with facts and figures rather than grief and emotion.

Your Therapist or Counselor

Your therapist or counselor is a critical member of your support team. She can help you understand and cope with your situation, whatever it is. A good therapist can assist you in moving forward with your life. Whether you want the divorce or not, you are in the process and a therapist can help you discover little pockets of peace. On your own, this can be very difficult.

A good therapist is worth the time and money she will cost. One therapist I know believes divorce is more painful for children than the death of a parent. Include your children and your husband in counseling sessions, if appropriate. It is vitally important that you learn how to support yourself and your children emotionally as well as financially. Counseling is particularly important if your marriage is ending because your husband has entered a new relationship. This creates special challenges because the betrayal adds a painful layer to the proceedings. It is a very difficult situation to manage. Strategic thinking is important and you may need extra support in making decisions.

In this instance, I believe it is important to act quickly. Your husband may be feeling guilty, which could put you in a good bargaining position. I've seen women wait one or two years to implement their divorces when their husbands were having affairs. Usually, these women don't fare as well as they might have. By then, their husbands have moved on and just want to finalize the divorce. They aren't feeling guilty any longer, they are feeling angry that their soon to be ex-wives are dragging their feet. This is not a good situation to be in and it weakens your position.

Steps to a Successful Divorce

Here are five strategies you can use to minimize your anxiety and maximize your prospects for emerging from the divorce feeling whole.

1. Focus on yourself and what you are doing rather than on your husband and his activities. Even though you are curious about his life now that you are no longer living together, don't ask him questions or try to find out where he is and what he is doing. Maintain your personal integrity and boundaries.

2. Cooperate with your husband as much as you can. Working together will help you create the best possible outcome for both of you, during and after the divorce. Make sure you take care of yourself in the process. Don't let him bully you or make you feel as if you don't know what you are doing.

3. Don't talk to him about the property settlement until you know exactly what there is, what you need, and what you want. When you talk with your husband about the settlement prior to the agreement, you weaken yourself. Recognize that your husband is no longer your friend, confidant, or financial advisor. It is better to wait until you, your financial advisor, and your lawyer have agreed upon a plan. Then present it to your husband, most likely through his lawyer. This helps to keep any destructive emotions in check.

4. This is a good time to look at your husband exactly as he is. Don't expect him to change much during the divorce process. If he hasn't been particularly supportive or generous during your marriage, it is highly unlikely he will be that way now. Try to assess how he is going to behave in this transaction. Think about how he views other business deals. This will give you important clues. Try to assess how your husband views you. Does he believe you are competent with money? Does he believe you will negotiate fairly? Does he believe you are strong or weak? Answering these questions will help you know what to expect from your husband.

5. Talk to your husband about the children and the day-to-day details. Do not talk to him about your future. Keep the details of your plans to yourself.

Dividing the Assets

Once you know what you want, decide where you can negotiate and where you can't. Know your bottom line and don't budge from it, even if your husband gets angry. If it's fair, he'll get over it. If it isn't fair, make it fair. You don't want to take advantage of him, you just want to get your fair share—nothing less and nothing more.

Spousal Support

I am a firm believer in trading spousal support for assets. Take spousal support only as a last resort because if your ex-husband owes you money every month, he can still control you. There is nothing worse for your sense of self than going to the mailbox to look for a spousal support check. If the check is there, you feel relief. If it isn't there, you feel vulnerable and threatened.

To be fair, I must say that this is not true for every woman, but it is something to consider. I have seen many women who live happily on their spousal support and don't give it a second thought. If you can do this, go for it. You should know your husband well enough to know whether getting paid on time will be a problem. If you believe you are entitled to spousal support and you believe your husband will treat you fairly and respectfully by sending the check on time, by all means ask for spousal support.

If this isn't the case, however, try to come up with another plan for generating cash. If you enjoy a net worth that can produce enough income for you to live on, that is a great alternative to spousal support. You can work out a formula to make sure you get enough of the investments or retirement plans to provide you with the income you need. This will work because you will have a sufficient amount of money to take care of your needs. Getting money is always better than getting a *promise* of money. Note that child support usually doesn't have the same negative impact on a woman that spousal support does. Child support is for your children. It ends when they are emancipated. Many states have laws on their books that will help you get your child support payments regularly and on time.

Rebuilding Your Life

Once the property settlement is negotiated, then your real work begins. Take time to reassess. Review your expense statement and make decisions based upon the amount of money you have. Be gentle and firm with yourself. Don't overspend. You don't want to run out of money later on. Living your life as if nothing has changed until your spousal and child support stop or until the investments run out can result in tragedy as you get older. When the support stops, it stops. Make sure you will be able to take care of yourself when this happens. You can either get a job or live on your investment income. Use your time and money wisely. Plan ahead and take good care of yourself.

And Now for the Good News

If you are single, you are in a perfect position to focus on your life and determine what you want and how you want to live. You have access to freedom you may have never experienced before. You are free to express yourself in all areas of your life. You can create the life you want. Now is the time to be bold and courageous. Make the most of it. Learn to be successful as a single person. Concentrate on making yourself whole. Focus on your future and leave your past behind. Do not anesthetize yourself with another relationship. Give yourself time to heal first.

As time goes by, you may slowly learn to appreciate your husband and the lessons you learned while you were with him. You may even begin to feel gratitude to your husband for the growth experience of your marriage. Of course, if you are in the middle of a divorce as you read this, you probably will be shaking your head in disbelief at the thought of ever feeling gratitude for your marriage and divorce. But, if you have already come through a divorce with your integrity intact and you are taking good care of yourself, you know exactly what I mean.

Single by Chance or by Choice

After your divorce you will be in a wonderful position because you can create your life exactly as you want it to be. Today, more women are single than ever before. Between 1970 and 1998, the number of women living alone doubled from 7.3 million to 15.3 million (U.S. Dept. of Commerce 2000).

Hopefully, you have a solid financial plan for managing your money. Your financial plan can assume you will be single for the rest of your life. If you do marry or enter into a partnership, you will be better off because you have been taking care of yourself. A new marriage doesn't mean that you won't have to pay attention to your money anymore. But it may mean you can live a more luxurious life because there will be more money available with two incomes instead of one. Prince Charming may be charming but he may not be very good at managing money, especially your money.

Many single women work in low paying jobs and find it difficult to pay their bills. They live paycheck to paycheck. They never seem to have the money to invest for the future. If you are single, it is essential to manage your money properly because you don't have another income as a fallback position. You should try to increase your income and reduce your expenses so that you can invest for your future. If you make this your goal, you can achieve it by staying conscious of what you want and setting an intention to have it.

On the other hand, many single women are well-paid executives or professionals who enjoy large incomes and retirement benefits. Many such women take very good care of themselves. Many don't. If, as a single person, you are earning good money, manage it as if your future depends upon it, because it does.

When Your Husband Dies

A woman is much more likely to live alone than a man. Almost half the women over sixty-five years old in the United States in 1997 were widows. About 70 percent of them live alone (AARP 1999). There were four times as many widows as widowers. That number increases with age. In fact, three of every five women age eighty-five or older, live alone or outside a family setting (U.S. Dept. of Commerce 1998). Men over sixty-five are much more likely to be married than women of the same age. Seventy-five percent of men versus 43 percent of women are still living with their spouses.

Losing your husband is a terrible experience. If you are a new widow, take the time you need to become stabilized before you make any big life changes. If you have the financial resources, stay put for at least one year. But then, it will be the time to move into a new life as a single woman. You don't want to stay stuck in your transition from wife to widow. Move on slowly if you must, but move on.

It is easier to come to terms with your loss when you are willing to move forward. Treading water, pretending that life is going on as usual is a mistake. Focusing on the family finances is a good place to start. You may discover a sense of power and freedom you didn't have during your marriage. Taking control can remove some of the sting from grief.

If you haven't been involved with your family's investments in the past, educate yourself as quickly as possible. Many widows are afraid to change the investments in their husbands' portfolios. You may not want to change the overall investment strategy, but you do want to understand your investments and you do want to be sure that they make sense for you in your new life.

If you turn to someone else for help, a son, a brother-in-law, or your husband's business partner, pay close attention and learn for yourself. Make sure those who are helping you understand what they are doing. Be sure to participate in any decision making so you don't seem childlike either to your financial advisor or to your children (who may want to tell you what to do).

Some widows who did not pay attention to money matters when their husbands were alive become terrified when their income stops and there is no money to pay the bills. They never realized they were financially vulnerable. In such a case, there is no time to waste. If this describes your situation, get a job and get it fast. Learn everything you can about managing money and create a new, financially secure life for yourself. It may take time, but it can be done.

If you are reading this chapter with a divorce looming or if you have been recently widowed, you have my deepest, heartfelt support. Divorce and death are never easy to cope with, but either can be an opportunity for you to grow and participate in the world in a new, exciting way.

CHAPTER SEVEN

SPENDING MONEY ON PURPOSE

Thinking is easy, acting is difficult, and to put one's thoughts into actions is the most difficult thing in the world.

Johann Wolfgang von Goethe (1749–1832)

Money can create magic in your life when you use it purposefully. Spending money should be joyful. Try to remember a time when you saw something in a store that called out to you—it seemed as if it was made just for you. It was the perfect color, size, and style. Just thinking about that time probably makes you smile.

To identify internally with something from the material world can be a wonderful feeling. It is this feeling you want to experience when you spend your money. After you have paid for all of the necessities, you want to feel that everything else you purchase expresses who you are. Maybe it doesn't appeal to any of your friends or family but it speaks to you. This is all that matters. After all, it is your money.

If you are like most people, you spend money from habit. You buy a soda at the same place at the same time. You don't even question whether you really *want* a soda, you just buy one. You buy your clothes at the same stores year after year. You don't even think about it. It's just what you do. There is nothing wrong with this. In fact, it is quite efficient. You just go along doing what you do. But if you are going to change your relationship to money, and manage it in a conscious way, you need to think about whether your habitual shopping habits work for you. They may not for two reasons:

1. You don't enjoy the process of shopping because you do it without thinking. It is difficult to enjoy things when you are not paying attention. You feel more enjoyment when you are actively engaged in your experience.

2. You may be buying things you don't really want just because they are available. This unconscious spending sometimes creates feelings of guilt.

Spending with a sense of purpose keeps you centered and in control of your money. Spending from habit or obligation keeps you stuck and anxious. Thinking consciously about everything you buy will help you to create a peaceful relationship with the material world.

Examining Your Spending

To find out whether you make your spending decisions in a conscious way or out of habit, examine how you behave, not what you say. Get out your check register and go through it. Or scan your credit card bills. You want to know where you are spending your money:

- *Are you expressing your values with your money?*

- *Are you spending more money than you have?*

- *Are you spending consciously or from habit?*

If you are spending money unconsciously, you may have some very good reasons for that. You may be angry about money. You may spend to get even with someone. If this sounds familiar, you are using money as a weapon rather than a tool. You may spend money to make yourself feel better about yourself and your life. You may be using money as a drug. If this is your situation, perhaps it would be wiser to spend your money on therapy. Once you acknowledge what you are doing, you can make different choices.

There is no point in judging or feeling shame about your relationship with money. Your goal is to observe your behavior so you can make better choices from now on. If you are too hard on yourself, you are more likely to stay stuck in your struggle to change. Release the judgment and you may find room to change your behavior. Just begin to pay attention to how and why you spend your money every single day.

It isn't what you buy, it's why you buy it that counts. It isn't the amount you spend, it's why you spend it that makes the difference. The price you pay for an item is irrelevant as long as your purchase gives you a sense of satisfaction and delight. As stated earlier in chapter 4, "cheap" and "expensive" are relative terms that don't have much objective meaning. If you find something you truly want and it is something that will give you pleasure, either as a memory or as an object, buy it, providing you can pay for it. If you cannot pay for something, it is too expensive no matter how much it costs.

You can afford to buy something if you meet the following conditions:

1. You have the money to pay cash or you can pay off your credit card if you use it for the purchase.

2. You are current with all of your bills and other expenses.

3. You have already put the maximum amount into your retirement plans and IRAs.

4. You have an adequate savings account, depending upon your circumstances.

5. You invest at least ten percent of your take-home pay in a taxable investment account.

When you have the basics covered, you are free to spend the rest on whatever makes you happy. If you do not yet have the basics covered, you can save up the money for an extravagant purchase. The goal is to spend your money intentionally.

A Conscious Spending Plan

Once you are aware of what you want to create for yourself, you can create your personal spending plan. I like to use the term "spending plan" rather than "budget" because a spending plan seems more positive. It says, "Here are the resources I have and this is how I choose to use them." The term "budget" carries a negative connotation to me. It sounds limiting. It says, "I cannot have." This may be a an idiosyncratic usage. However, I encourage you to take a consciously positive approach to everything concerning money, including the language you use to think about it as well as how you intend to spend it. Remember that money management takes place every single day, every single time you choose to buy something or not. All money management starts with how you are currently using your money. It is impossible to determine how much money you need until you know how much money you spend.

$ Think About It . . .

Treat yourself to a money management weekend. Plan to spend several hours gaining clarity about your relationship with money. Find a quiet place to do your work. Relax and enjoy the process. It's an important time for you. You are taking control of your life by assessing how you spend your money.

- *First, find a few months or a year's worth of credit card statements, check stubs, and all of the receipts and information that will give you a picture of your total spending. In the first column, starting at the top of the page, list your spending categories such as mortgage, taxes, heat, utilities (by type), food, insurance, etc. You want to really understand what you are doing with your money, so the more categories you have, the better. Across the top of the paper, write the months, beginning with the month that just passed. (See Total Spending Chart below for a model.)*

- *Then just start filling in the numbers and adding up the categories month by month. If you have more than $25 a month in any one area, make a new category so you can get an accurate picture. For example, if you buy more than $25 worth of books each month, list books as a separate category. If you spend more than $25 every month on manicures, list them separately and so on. The more precisely you look at your spending habits, the better estimates you will have. A big miscellaneous category is not helpful.*

- *Then add up your fixed expenses separately from your variable or discretionary expenses. Fixed expenses are items such as your mortgage or rent, property taxes, utilities, etc. They are bills you must pay no matter what. Variable or discretionary expenses are those where you can choose to make purchases or not. This includes items such as clothes, groceries, and entertainment. Obviously, you need to buy groceries, but you have discretion over where you shop and how much you spend. This is contrary to paying for heat or water. If you want those items, you must pay the bill, no matter how much it is.*

* *If you pay your insurance premiums quarterly or twice a year, divide the annual premium by twelve so you know how much you need each month to cover that expense. Use the same strategy with holidays, gifts, and taxes. Determine how much you spend annually on these items and divide the amount by twelve. This will give you an accurate monthly number to work with. This is helpful because you can more easily match it to your income, which is probably received on a regular basis.*

* *If you don't have a regular income, you can keep track of the seasonal expenses and compare them to your income projections. The idea is for you to have the money to pay your bills when they are due.*

* *If you have all of your expenses on a computer program, you can use those figures. But writing it down with pencil and paper will help you access the information. You will gain clarity and greater understanding when you write it down than if you look at computer printouts. Computers don't manage your money, you do. Computers can help you, but they are no substitute for your own mind and creativity.*

Adding the Extras

When you finish the exercise above, you will know how much money you need to keep going every month. You also want to cover extras that take a lump sum, such as buying a car, painting your house, or taking a trip. These are not part of your ongoing spending plan. They belong in a separate category. For example, list everything you can think of that you want to do to your home, such as carpets, a new roof, or building a fence. Then find out how much each item will cost. It's important to find out what something costs because you may be going without something you want that is relatively inexpensive and easy for you to buy now.

I have a friend who wanted a rubber sprayer on her kitchen faucet for years. But she consistently talked herself out of it by saying she didn't really need it. She had the notion that she couldn't really afford it because it was a luxury. She was dumbfounded to learn the item cost $1.29. She couldn't believe that she had allowed herself to want something for so long that was so easily affordable because she

Sample Spending Plan *

Item	Jan	Feb	Mar	April	May	June	July	Aug	Sept	Oct	Nov	Dec †
Mortgage												
Property Taxes												
Garbage												
Heat												
Telephone												
Electricity												
Groceries												
Restaurants												
Home Insurance												
Car Insurance												
Gasoline												
Clothing												
Groceries												
Total	$	$	$	$	$	$	$	$	$	$	$	$

* These are just a few items you will have on your spending plan. Be sure to include categories such as gifts, dry cleaning, pets, personal care, etc.

† $\div$ 12 = monthly expenses

hadn't checked it out. If you want something you think you can't have, make sure you check out the price. It may not cost as much as you think it does.

Your spending got you where you are today. Spending will also determine where you are tomorrow. Keep in mind that spending money is not about budgeting. It is about making conscious choices. As you evaluate your relationship with money, you might want to change your spending, saving, and investing habits. You will gradually figure these matters out through your process of self-discovery. Give yourself the time you need to think things through and to learn how to gracefully maneuver in the world of money.

Cut Up Your Credit Cards

A chapter about spending wouldn't be complete without a discussion of consumer debt. If your examination of your spending patterns reveals that you spend money on interest, read on. If you do not carry debt, except for a mortgage or a car payment, good for you. You can skip this part of the chapter.

Credit cards have their place in your financial life. They are convenient to use. They allow you to buy something today and pay for it in a few weeks. They provide you with a record of your purchases. It is fine to have and use credit cards as long as you pay off the balance every month. It is not a good idea to use credit cards and carry a balance.

If a certain portion of your money goes toward paying off credit cards and other time payments, you may not have enough money to buy things you really want. Managing your money when you have debt makes the job more difficult. However, it is possible to get out of debt. Determine to do that as quickly as possible. Many conscientious women are in trouble because of debt. The debt they have accumulated puts the quality of their lives at risk for the following reasons: debt creates anxiety, relationship problems, and financial chaos.

Debt Creates Anxiety

Women who carry debt usually tell me they have no sense of getting ahead or of accomplishing anything. They feel discouraged and cheated because they work very hard and have "nothing to show for it." Sometimes, they believe their financial problems are insurmountable, and frequently they lack the motivation to pay off their debt because they are too frightened to face the financial situation they have created. They feel shame about not being financially astute. They also feel depressed and angry, and despair of ever getting ahead. They live in a constant state of anxiety.

Debt Creates Relationship Problems

Some women hide their debt from partners, spouses, or other important people in their lives. They live in constant fear that they will be found out. They overspend because they feel the social pressure to keep up with their friends. But they can't be truly intimate with their friends because their feelings of guilt, shame, and fear prevent them from self-disclosing. They tell me they worry endlessly about what will happen when their debt is discovered.

They don't know how they can ever get out of debt because they can't be honest about it. This puts them in a terrible position because their secret prevents them from taking action. They continue to pretend their finances are okay at great personal cost to themselves and their relationships. If they continue in these self-destructive behaviors, they completely destroy their peace of mind and their relationships. Many women carrying heavy debt experience feelings of anger and resentment toward others. They are envious of friends who seem to have everything they want without using credit cards. They may fail to understand the principle that those who don't pay interest have more money to spend.

It is so easy to get into debt and so difficult to eliminate. Sometimes it actually destroys a marriage or partnership. Several times a year I see couples who are at the point of breaking up because they cannot agree on how to manage their debt. The individual parties feel such anxiety that they can't continue the relationship. Each may blame the other person for creating their financial nightmare. Their use of debt to finance their lifestyle literally snuffs the life out of their relationship.

Debt Creates Financial Chaos

Some women saddled with heavy debt often rob Peter to pay Paul. Of course, they are both Peter and Paul. They spend their time worrying about how to get out of debt. Often, they can't buy the things they want because they don't have a good credit rating. Sometimes, their bad credit keeps them from getting a job they want, so they miss out on opportunities to get ahead.

They can't seem to ever move forward. They just seem to keep afloat. This is because they are virtually throwing their money down the drain. They are buying interest and interest is basically "nothing." So they buy "nothing" and they have "nothing" to show for it. Their debt mortgages their future and their present. They can't invest because their investment dollars are paying the interest charges. It's a vicious cycle that goes on and on.

It has occurred to me that some women get away with not managing their money properly while they are younger. Just as they can get away with not taking care of their bodies or their faces. This is true for women in their twenties, thirties, and well into their forties. But by the time they reach age fifty, it shows. If they haven't take care of their money, very likely they don't have many assets. They have no idea how they can ever retire. They are afraid of the future. If they own a house, it is in a state of disrepair because they can't afford to take care of it. They often drive old beater cars because they don't have the money for maintenance and repairs. They have my heartfelt sympathy because they are scared and they are looking at a rather bleak future. If they are married or partnered, usually they are having difficulties in the relationship because both parties are scared and they don't have anywhere to turn. It's a very difficult situation.

Changing Your Mind About Debt

If you identify with any of the scenarios described above, I assure you there is hope! You can get out of debt if you want to. You just have to set an intention to change your mind and your actions. You have to determine what you want and how you want to get there. When you decide to get out of debt, miracles do happen.

Winning the Lottery Isn't the Answer

It is very unlikely that you are in debt because you don't have enough money. It is more likely you are in debt because you don't manage the money you have very well. Of course, this is not always the case. You may be in debt because of sudden catastrophic circumstances such as severe illness or job loss. However, this kind of debt is easier to handle because it was created by an emergency rather than by misusing credit.

Even if you managed to pay off your credit cards with a windfall, such as an inheritance, if you haven't dealt with the underlying reasons for your debt, you might go right back into debt again. At first, you would feel great and your anxiety would be gone because you were debt-free. But once your anxiety lifted, you would be very likely to build up the debt again unless you understood why you were in debt in the first place.

You might be thinking of using the equity in your home to pay off your credit cards. I caution against this practice. If you use your home equity, either by refinancing your home or with a second mortgage, you are using an asset to pay for current consumption. This is not a good thing to do because your home may be the biggest investment you have. It doesn't make much sense anyway. Think about it. If you refinance your home with a thirty-year mortgage to pay off credit cards, you will be paying for your clothes or dining out or a vacation for the next thirty years.

I have talked with many women who have paid off all their credit cards time and time again and keep building up their debt again and again. I've also talked with clients who have declared bankruptcy two and three times. These people have paid off their debt, but they never examined and dealt with the underlying reason for the debt. If this is you, I encourage you to take action today.

Getting Out of Debt for Good

Getting out of debt is a worthy goal. Often debt is the biggest reason that women don't feel successful. If you have to borrow money to make purchases, you probably don't feel very good either about yourself or your purchases. So, let's take a look at another way to live. The first place to start is to tell the truth about your debt. You need to know everything about it. Telling the truth may be difficult because facing the truth can feel frightening. Just take a deep breath and add up the total. Once you know how much debt you have, you can work with it. If you don't know how much debt you have, you can't get it under control.

Personal Debt

There are two kinds of debt, personal and institutional. Personal debt is money borrowed from friends and family. Sometimes money borrowed from friends and family costs the highest price imaginable. You can lose the relationship because of the debt. If you borrow money from your friends or relatives, make sure you both agree that it is a business transaction. Sign a note that spells out the amount of the loan, the interest rate, and the payment terms. Make the payments on time and pay off the debt as soon as you can. Even if the loan isn't mentioned when you see your friends and relatives, it has an adverse effect on the relationship.

Institutional Debt

Credit card companies and banks issue institutional debt. Institutional debt includes credit card balances, student or school loans, car loans, home equity loans and lines of credit, margin loans against securities when not used to purchase securities, bank loans and lines of credit, loans from retirement plans such as 401(k) loans, and loans from the cash value of your life insurance.

Good Debt

When you are reviewing your loans, keep in mind that there are times when borrowing money is the smart thing to do. For example, you can borrow money for a short time before you will receive money promised to you. If you are starting a new business, you may need to borrow money. You may want to borrow money to repair your car or house if you don't have the cash. Or you may have an illness or family emergency that requires money you don't have.

Student Loans

Student loans provide an interesting dilemma. If you are thinking about going back to school on borrowed money, there are a few factors that should be taken into consideration. For example, if you are learning a new skill or getting a degree that will help you to increase your income, going back to school is likely to be a good investment in your future. In this case, you know you will create the money to pay back the loans in record time. Note that the younger you are, the better.

If you are over age fifty and thinking of going back to school on borrowed money, be very careful. After you graduate, or get your certificate, you may not be able to generate enough income in the marketplace to pay back your loans. I've met some women who will never be able to pay off their student loans and they feel very discouraged. If you plan to go back to school on credit, research the job market in your field and make sure you won't be crushed by the loans. Write a plan to pay off the loan before you act. What will your income and expenses be after graduation? How long will it take to pay off those loans? Are your income projections realistic? Don't forget to add your living expenses into the calculations. Is it worth it to you? If you borrow money consciously and for a good reason, you are very likely to pay it back without too much trouble. The difference between good debt and bad debt lies in the reason for the debt in the first place.

Interest: The Cost of Money

When you are assessing your debt, think of the interest you pay as the cost of money. How much does money cost? The higher the interest rate, the higher the cost of money. You can determine if you want to borrow money by assessing the reason for borrowing versus the cost of borrowing.

I recently purchased a new car. I borrowed the money because the interest rate, or the cost of borrowing, was rather low. I could have taken the money out of my stock portfolio and paid cash for the car, but I was getting higher returns in the market. So, I chose car payments. After a few months, I decided to pay off my car loan by using the margin in my stock portfolio. The collateral for my car isn't the car, it is my stocks. Basically, I make a car payment to my investment account. Rather than making a car payment to a bank, I make it to myself. I figured this out on paper and over the five years of the car loan, I am several thousand dollars ahead. This assumes, of course, that my stock market projections are on target.

The reason I cite this example is so you can see that managing your money includes managing debt. As stated above, there are times when going into debt makes sense and times when it is disastrous. Know the difference. A good rule is to use debt to finance only assets, such as a house or an education. Do not use debt to buy anything that will be used up before you get the bill. This will keep you from putting frivolous and unnecessary items on your credit cards. Consciously using debt doesn't keep you awake nights. You will know you have debt and you will know why. You will have made an educated, conscious choice. It makes all the difference.

The best test is to examine how your debt makes you feel. If you feel satisfied when you use a credit card, you are probably using debt wisely. (Hopefully, you are using the credit card for convenience and pay it off every month.) If you feel anxious and upset before, during, or after a credit card transaction, what needs to change?

Write Down the Reasons for Your Debt

Strange as this may sound, you may be addicted to managing your debt problems. If you are constantly thinking about your debt and figuring out various payment scenarios, you may be living in a "comfort zone" of debt-anxiety. You may come from a family where debt is normal. Personally, I believe that debt is hereditary. You can get it from your parents. It isn't carried in the genes, but it is learned by observing your parents' behavior. If your parents are in debt, you may be following the same path. But you can make a different choice. I will never forget Lauren, a thirty-four-year-old woman, saying that the reason she came to a workshop was because "I have a feeling my parents are still paying for my baby clothes and I don't want to repeat the cycle."

If you have a propensity to go in and out of debt, figure out what being in debt does for you. It must work for you in some manner or you wouldn't continue to spend more money than you have. If you can't figure it out, talk to a therapist or counselor about it. This would be a very good use of your money. Go back to chapter 3 and figure out how to change your mind about being in debt.

Examine your feelings about your debt. Pay attention to your body when you think about your debt. Notice your feelings when you use your credit card against your better judgment. Common feelings are anger and resentment, shame or embarrassment, helplessness, and apathy. Observe that these are feelings of powerlessness. You can change your feelings by changing your behavior and you can change your behavior by changing your feelings. If your feelings make you uncomfortable, try not to rationalize your debt with the thought that "everybody is in debt." This may be true, but "everybody who is in debt" will face the music one day.

 Think About It . . . .

Note your thoughts and feelings as you buy things on credit that you know you can't pay for when the bill comes. This may help you figure out what being in debt does for you. You might want to talk with a therapist or counselor about it. You could even attend Debtor's Anonymous meetings so you can share your challenges with people in similar circumstances.

Now, in your journal, write the answers to the following questions:

- *How do you feel about paying interest?*
- *How do you feel about paying late fees?*
- *What else could you have done with the money?*
- *Do you remember what you've bought on credit?*

- *Do you still want and use the items?*
- *What else can you do with your money if you are not paying interest?*
- *Are you willing to invest the money you would have paid in interest?*
- *If you invested it and earned 10 percent, how much would it be in ten years?*
- *When will you be debt-free?*

The High Cost of Credit

When you buy on credit, your money is not working for you in any way. That is why people who use credit and pay interest usually wind up with nothing later in life. Young couples who start out using credit cards find it very difficult to build any net worth over their lifetimes. Living on credit becomes a way of life that is very disheartening and unsatisfying. Most people can't even remember what they spent the money on!

Sherry, a thirty-two-year-old realtor I know, got a VISA card in the mail and decided to use it to buy a new state-of-the-art sound system. She spent $3,500 and just loves the system. The interest rate, at 16.5 percent on the card, is a little less than her other cards, which is great. Money is tight for her, but she always manages to make the minimum payment. She doesn't like to be in debt, though, and she cut up the VISA card and will never use it again.

If Sherry dutifully makes all of the minimum payments on her credit card, she will pay her debt off when she is eighty years old. It will take her forty-eight years. By then, her state-of-the-art sound system will be an antique. She will have paid over $41,000 in interest. She will also have given up the opportunity loss she incurred by spending the money rather than investing it. (An opportunity loss is the very real loss of that not chosen when you choose one path over another. For example, if you go to the beach instead of the mountains, you miss an opportunity to see the beach. All choices carry an opportunity loss, because all choices involve a choice to do one thing as well as a choice to not do something else.)

If Sherry had invested the $3,500 at ten percent for forty-eight years, she would have earned $339,560. *This story illustrates the high cost of credit. There are numerous methods to determine the cost of credit that may not give you these exact figures. But the message is always clear. It is difficult to pay off credit card debt when you make only the minimum payments. If you want to pay off your credit cards, pay more than the minimum each month and you will cut the number of years dramatically.*

Credit Card Basics

Credit cards are great for keeping track of your financial transactions, for emergencies, and for getting credit. Sometimes they are more convenient than carrying cash. There is a lag time between your purchase and the time the payment is due so you get to use other people's money for a few weeks. However, using credit is a good deal only if you use it responsibly. The credit card companies have all the cards stacked in their favor. They want to keep you hooked on credit. That's how they make money.

There are four basic factors to consider when choosing a credit card. They are as follows:

1. **Interest Rate**. This is referred to as an annual percentage rate or APR. It's shown on the back of your statement. You want to pay off those cards that have the highest APR first. You may pay a higher interest rate for cash advances than you do for purchases. Interest rates are tricky, so read the fine print. This is your money, so pay attention.

2. **Grace Period**. This is the amount of time you have to pay for the items you charge on the card. In some cases, it can be only as short as ten days or so. Be very careful here because some credit card companies don't offer a grace period unless you pay the balance in full every month.

3. **Late Fees**. If you don't get your payment in on time, you'll be charged a late fee in addition to the interest. You might also be charged a fee if you go over your credit limit. Note that the credit card companies' fees keep increasing. They know most of their customers aren't paying attention, so they do exactly what they want to do. They know you don't have the money to pay your bill or you would.

4. **Annual Fee**. This is a charge for the privilege of using the credit card. The fee ranges from $15 to $100 yearly. Note that many companies don't charge an annual fee.

All credit cards are not created equal. There are various strategies for using credit cards, depending upon your spending habits. If you pay off the charges monthly within the grace period (usually around twenty days), the annual fee is your most important consideration. This holds true if you occasionally carry very small balances. If you carry a balance of more than $300 every month, then the annual percentage rate (APR) is more important to you. You might want to carry two cards—one with low fees you can pay off monthly for smaller purchases, and one with a low APR where you intend to carry a balance forward.

Investing While Paying Off Credit Is a Good Idea

You may be wondering if you should use all of your extra money to pay down your credit cards or if you should invest at the same time. This is a difficult question because of the time-value of money. The more time you have, the more your money will grow. If it takes you several years to pay off your debt, that is several years that your money won't be working for you if you don't invest it. So, you need to think of both things at once by including investing in your debt-management plan.

Your spending plan will determine how much money you have to pay on your credit cards. Put the largest share of that money toward your debt, at least 75 percent. The rest should be invested for your future. Your money needs to grow over the years you are reducing your debt. And it doesn't take much. You could, for example, pay $150 on your credit cards and invest $50. Increase your investments as your credit balances drop.

Credit Reporting Agencies

A good credit rating is an essential part of everyone's financial life. It can make a sudden emergency easier to deal with. Make sure you know what is in your credit reports. Many people who are in debt are afraid to look at their own credit reports. Facing the truth of where you are with your credit is a big step in getting your credit issues squared away.

Get a credit report from at least one credit reporting agency once a year, just so you know what is being reported on your behalf. Credit reporting agencies are notorious for making mistakes in mixing people up or not getting up-to-date information on payments.

Keep in mind that all of your credit cards appear on your report, even if you don't use them. They are included in the total amount of credit you carry for loan purposes. The fewer credit cards you have, the less likely you are to experience credit reporting problems. Be sure you understand how to correct any mistakes on your credit report. Also, talk with the credit reporting agency and your creditors to see if you can clear up any negative entries. There are three main credit reporting companies. Contact one or all of the following, depending upon your need. Experian @ 1-800-682-7654, Equifax @ 1-800-685-1111, or Trans Union @ 1-800-916-8800.

Planning Your Debt-Free Future

Here are eight easy steps for eliminating your debt. If you follow them, you will create a debt-free future.

1. **Decide you want to get out and stay out of debt.** This is the most important part of the process. Debt elimination starts in your mind. You may need to negotiate with your partner/ spouse so they will support you in your determination.

2. **Stop using credit cards immediately.** Use only one credit card that you pay off every month. This will help you build the habit of using a credit card wisely.

3. **Determine where you stand right now.** List all your debt. Look inside to discover the underlying reasons for your debt, both personal and institutional.

4. **Contact your creditors if you can't make your payments on time.** Call them if you are having a problem making the payments. Always call before you miss a payment and tell them why you are missing the payment and what you are going to do about it. Or you can write your creditors explaining the situation. Whether you call or write you must contact your creditors. It is your responsibility to communicate with them. Also, be sure to ask them to reduce the interest rate. They may agree to reduce it or they may not, but at least you will have made the effort.

5. **Make a written plan and stick to it.** You will do much better with a written plan than without one. It is much easier to manage money when you write things down rather than trying to do all the sums in your head.

6. **Stick to your plan even when you don't feel like it.** Recognize that old habits are difficult to break and don't become discouraged if you slip. Acknowledge your setback and get back on track. Realize that it might take several years to become completely debt-free.

7. **Tell the people close to you that you are committed to getting out of debt.** Enlist their support. Your friends may learn from your honesty. You may be doing them a favor. Talking about it also helps to alleviate some of the shame and anxiety you may feel. If you let your indebtedness out of the closet, you feel better.

8. **Don't put anything on a credit card that will be consumed before you get the bill.** This means food, vacations, and entertainment.

9. **Watch the closing date.** Manage your cash flow by making purchases after the monthly closing date.

A Simple Payment Plan

The trick is to come up with a manageable payment plan and stick to it. Always make more than the minimum payment on every single card if you can. Pay any extra money that might come your way to the card that charges the highest rate of interest. Keep repeating this process.

Don't worry. If you follow a manageable payment plan consistently, you will get out of debt. Your payment plan and your intention to get yourself out of debt will get you out of debt. I've seen women who felt hopelessly indebted become debt-free almost miraculously. Setting the intention and following it with action somehow sets a miracle in motion. Clients have called me to say they got a raise, or a bonus, or someone paid back a long-lost loan. The money seems to follow the intention. Give yourself permission to enjoy the present because you are getting out of debt. The process is in motion. Good for you.

Staying Out of Debt

1. **Think about your spending.** Make daily spending choices out of conscious intention rather than habit. Make choices that are consistent with your desire to get out of debt. Under-

stand that you always have a choice and make choices that support you.

2. **Identify wants versus needs**. Many people have their wants and needs mixed up. You need food, clothing, shelter, and water. You can spend a lot or a little on these needs. You want cars, televisions, motorcycles, and cell phones. Buy all of what you need and only some of what you want. Also, determine the one want that makes you feel life is worth living and make sure you get it. But ignore your other wants in favor of your real desire, which is to get out of debt.

3. **Compare your need for instant gratification to your long-term goals**. Eat at home so you can pay off your bills. Take short, inexpensive vacations so you can go to Europe when your debt is paid. Start a "pent-up demand list." Don't make impulse purchases. Give yourself a "cooling off" period before buying anything except necessities. Think about something you really want and go back and buy it if you still want it, knowing that it will take you that much longer to pay off your debt.

4. **Don't shop for recreation**. Stay away from the malls and stay out of the stores. Find a hobby that doesn't cost money. Don't be coerced to shop by friends or family. Borrow, don't buy. For example, use the library to find the books you want to read. Only buy books you want to own. Borrow CDs and videos from the library. Ask friends if you can borrow things you may need—and make sure you return them.

5. **Shop in your closet**. Find new outfits by putting clothes together in a new way. Go to resale shops. Wear the same thing two days in the same week. You don't need to impress others by the number of outfits you have. If you are appropriately dressed, that's all that counts.

6. **Eat at home regularly**. Use restaurants only for special occasions. Take your lunch to work. Cook on weekends so you always have food to eat during the week when you might be too tired to fix dinner. Entertain friends at home rather than going to a restaurant. Watch the bar bills.

When You Can't Keep Up with Your Payments

There are a few things you can do if you find yourself in a position where you cannot keep your payments current. Call your creditor first. Don't wait for them to contact you. You can discuss your situation and tell them where you are financially. Explain the reasons you can't keep up your payments and how you intend to pay them eventually.

Here are some options that are available to you:

1. Reduce your monthly payment to one you can afford.

2. Refinance the loan to get a better interest rate or better terms in general.

3. Defer payment for a short time if you expect to be able to pay soon.

4. Pay the interest only until you can resume monthly payments. At least you will be keeping up with the cost of the interest.

5. Sell the item and use the cash to satisfy, or partially satisfy, the debt.

6. Get a consolidation loan if all else fails. That is, borrow money on your house or from another source, and then pay off all of your big debts. This leaves you with one big loan rather than several small ones.

You do not want to lose your home, so contact your home mortgage lender immediately and discuss your situation. You could discuss a few of the following ideas to buy yourself time:

1. Pay interest only for a certain period of time.

2. Skip one or two payments.

3. Arrange for lower payments temporarily.

If your house payment is more than you will be able to afford for the forseeable future, think about renting a room or two for extra income. Or you can rent your house to someone else and find less costly housing for yourself. Another alternative would be to sell your house and buy or rent an apartment. Or you could move in with relatives or friends temporarily until you get back on your feet. If you are renting a house or apartment and you have fallen behind in your rent, make sure you talk to your landlord immediately and try to make arrangements for smaller payments until you can get caught up.

Put any plan you agree upon in writing . . . and follow it. Keep track of your discussions with creditors so you know what agreements you have made. Write down the names and phone numbers of the people whom you contacted. Keep track of the dates of your conversations and make notes about your discussions.

Potential Sources of Funds

You may want to review your assets and see if you can find money somewhere to pay off your bills. Of course, you are taking money from yourself, but the interest rate may be better. For example, you could borrow from your 401(k) plan at work, or you could borrow money from relatives. A few words of caution, though. Be sure you pay off your debts with the money. Be sure that you do not create any more debt. Make sure you pay back the money according to a preplanned debt repayment schedule.

The biggest drawback to borrowing from yourself is that you may not pay yourself back, or you may go out and put more money on your credit cards. If this is even a remotely possibility, don't do it! This goes for a home equity loan or refinancing your home. I wish you well in your quest to climb out of debt into financial freedom. You can do it just by making a conscious choice to spend your money consciously and with integrity. Go for it!

Chapter Eight

Planning Makes the Difference

A Number Two pencil and a dream can take you anywhere.

Joyce A. Myers (1948–)

You may be wondering how you can begin to make your money work for you. The most efficient way to use your time and energy when you are focusing on your money is to plan your success in writing. It is extremely difficult to manage money in your head. Writing things down benefits you in a variety of ways.

1. It gives you clarity. Just going through the process helps you understand what you have and what you need to do. You will very likely discover the best plan for yourself just by gathering the information and writing it down. The very act of writing helps you process your financial information.

   Writing things down gives your body information. Your body is a valuable tool that you can use to determine what you want and don't want in life. When you are faced with difficult or challenging questions about your money choices, you will find the answers by listening to your body. Your body will tell you when you are on the right track. For example, your stomach might feel tight or slightly queasy after you agree to pay for something that you know you can't afford. You will always feel a twinge somewhere if you aren't acting in your own best interest. Think of how different your body feels when you are being praised compared to times when you are being criticized. Learn to read your body and pay attention to the clues.

2. The act of writing strengthens your commitment. When you use time and energy to write your plan, on a subliminal, subconscious level you are you making a commitment to change. You are more likely to act on your plan when you have written it down. Somehow, writing things down creates impressions in your body that encourage you to act. You engage your whole being: mind, body, and soul when you consciously look at your finances and create a written plan.

3. Writing your financial situation out in detail causes you to become less emotional about your money. When you have a written financial plan, you don't have to spend time wondering what you should do. For example, if you have a written investment plan that you believe is well-crafted, you won't feel fearful when the stock market drops. You don't have to worry and obsess about the size of your debt when you have a written plan to become debt-free. You can be much more rational about money when you know your plan of action. This frees up your energy for other areas of your life.

An investment plan doesn't have to be pretty to be effective. You can write your first draft on the back of a scratch pad or an envelope. The crucial component is that you spend your time thoughtfully assessing your financial condition, and that you create a workable plan for making the most of your money.

Don't start writing your plan at your computer. Use a pencil and paper. You will have a better understanding of your current financial situation and your future alternatives if you sit down with pencil and paper rather than working at your computer. Writing down the numbers and adding them up is a sensory experience that helps you understand how to use the figures to create your action plan.

This is a plan you will want to review at least once a year, so it is more convenient to store it on your computer. But begin with a pad of paper, a pencil (not a pen because you will want to erase), and a calculator. Then transfer the information to your computer so you will have a legible, permanent record. When you do transfer your plan to a computer, you can use a spreadsheet, money management software, or even just a word processing format.

A Financial Plan Must Be Flexible

Your financial plan is always a work in process. You are never done, because your life is always changing. So you need to build flexibility into your plan, or you will not be very happy with it. For example, Sandra, a client of mine, has been diligently following her financial plan for at least a year. She called recently to tell me her favorite nephew is graduating from college and she wants to attend the ceremony, but her research indicated the trip would cost about $500. This was a bit much for her to spend. She said, "I can always drive to California to see him next summer." But, clearly, she was not happy with that solution, and she wanted to know if I had any other suggestions.

I asked her how many times her nephew was going to graduate with high honors. Of course, this was the only time. Then the solution came easily. She will use her credit card for traveling expenses and pay the card back with the $250 per month that she usually invests. This means she will not meet the goals of her investment plan by the end of the year. But she will always have the memory of going to the graduation celebration. She made a conscious choice. A family experience like this is worth the money.

This brings me to another point. Manage your money within the context of your life. No decision can be a purely financial decision. If you are managing your money based one hundred percent on the financial impact of your choices, I would guess that you do not live your life to the fullest. Be flexible. Decide to have all the life experiences that are important to you and you can still be true to your financial plan.

This philosophy holds true both for life experiences and one-of-a-kind purchases. We all experience times in our lives when we want something that may be thought of as frivolous or extravagant. Pay attention to your feelings during these times. If it is truly important to you, perhaps you can find a way to make it happen. You can tell by your body how important something is to you. If you feel happy and excited or deeply moved, it's important. If you think about something over and over, it's important. Obviously, you don't feel this way about most things. You may see many things you like, but very few things you absolutely love. It's not a good idea to buy everything you like, but it's a great idea to buy the few things that you just love. Your body will show you the difference.

Your Model Financial Profile

It is nearly impossible for anyone to tell you exactly where you should be financially at any of the various stages of life. However, I do think you might find it helpful to know what being on solid financial ground looks like. There are certain things you always want to have in place, no matter where you are in life:

1. You want and need adequate savings to cover emergencies and for opportunities.

2. You want and need to put money aside for your retirement and the future. (This is money that is usually tax-deferred, such as IRAs and employer retirement plans.)

3. You want and need to put money aside in a taxable long-term investment portfolio. (This is in addition to the money you are putting away for retirement. You can spend this money anytime without incurring any tax penalties.)

4. You want *no* consumer debt with the exception of a mortgage and possibly a car payment.

5. You want and need insurance that will protect you from any financial disasters that might arise. Note that your insurance needs change as the years go by.

6. You should always have an up-to-date will.

The Stages of Life

For most women these life stages are merely suggestions. I realize your circumstances may be very different from those I have outlined. If you have inherited wealth or are wealthy in your own right, you have additional considerations. Even so, you may benefit from reading this section.

Ages Twenty-five to Thirty-five

You are very likely earning a living in the marketplace and making plans for your future. This is a good time to start educating yourself about money, so that your money doesn't slip through your fingers. Take classes, read books on investing, and talk with your friends about how they manage their money. Learn all you can. Learn how to live today and take care of tomorrow.

Your Savings Account

If you keep a few thousand dollars in a savings account, you will be ahead when you have an emergency. If you have pets, a car, or own your home, you need more cash on hand than if you don't. Pets need care and cars and houses need repairs. You don't want to put these items on a credit card and pay interest.

Decide how much you want in your savings account and try to stay at that amount at all times. For example, if you have $2,500 in your savings account, and you use $600 for a vacation, try to pay the money back as soon as possible. If you don't have a savings account, open one at your bank or credit union or put cash into a mutual fund money market account. Add to your savings account every month until you reach the desired amount.

Financial advisors differ on the amount of money you need to have readily available to you. I think it depends upon your circumstances. If you are in a very stable job with a predictable income and steady expenses, you won't need as much in your savings account as you would in a volatile job or profession. If you are married or have a partner who has a separate income, you can reduce your savings according to the stability of your partner's financial circumstances. If you can live on one of your incomes, you are in a great position to keep a modest amount in your savings account and you can invest the rest.

Use your savings account to sock money away for special things. You might want to save for the down payment on a house, or a vacation, or a wedding. If you need money for any reason within the next five years, put it in your savings account. Don't invest it. The market is too volatile for you to invest money you will need. See chapter 9 for more details about saving and investing.

Retirement Plans

If your company has a retirement plan, such as a 401(k) plan, contribute as much as you possibly can. Read the communication materials you receive so that you understand the plan as well as the investments. If you can self-direct your investments, you very likely will have to choose from among a variety of mutual funds.

Many women don't invest aggressively enough. They are afraid they will lose their money. The younger you are, the more aggressive an investor you can be. Look into your alternatives and put together a rational portfolio based on solid research. (A "portfolio" is the term commonly used when referring to one's investments.) Do your homework. Don't take anybody else's suggestions without doing your own research. Take your investments seriously.

Time is an investor's best friend. The longer your money works for you, the more money you will have. You can invest rather aggressively when you are in your twenties and thirties because you have years ahead of you. You can put one hundred percent of your investments into a diversified portfolios of stocks. This is opposed to investing in bonds or fixed income investments.

If your company doesn't have a retirement plan, then open an Individual Retirement Account (IRA) and try to contribute the maximum allowed by the IRS every year. Consider opening a Roth IRA rather than a contributory IRA. A Roth IRA is a better deal for the long term. It grows tax-free because you can't deduct your contribution from your taxes. A contributory IRA grows tax-deferred because you may be able to deduct the annual contribution. This means you don't pay any taxes on the money you take from your Roth IRA and you do pay taxes on the money you take from your contributory IRA. The IRS has imposed salary guidelines for contributing to a Roth and the deductibility of a contributory IRA. Put money into an IRA even if you are covered under a retirement plan through your work. The more money you invest for your future, the better. Money in an IRA grows faster because of its favorable tax status even if you can't deduct it. Take advantage of it.

Contributory IRA	Roth IRA
You may deduct your annual contribution from your taxes.	You can't deduct your annual contribution from your taxes.
You do pay taxes when you take money from this kind of IRA.	You don't pay taxes when you take money from this kind of IRA.

There are various conditions that apply to IRAs. Talk with your accountant about it.

Children's College Fund

If you have children, you may want to start a college fund. The sooner you start putting money away for your kids' education, the easier it will be for you to send them to college. See if putting $500 a year into a college IRA makes sense for you.

I'm not a fan of putting your children's college money in trusts such as a uniform gifts to minors trust (UTMA). You may gain tax benefits, but you lose control of the money. With an UTMA, your child gets the money at age eighteen or twenty-one, depending upon your state's laws. The money doesn't have to be used for college. It is your child's money and can be used for any purpose. I think it is better when parents and children decide together how the money is to be used.

Insurance Needs

Make sure you have adequate health insurance coverage. Your health is your most important asset. Getting sick costs you time, money, and life energy. If you don't have any dependents, you don't need life insurance. Health and car insurance may be all you need at this time. If you own your home, you do need homeowner's insurance. If you rent, look into renter's insurance if you have personal items of value. You may want to purchase disability insurance, particularly if you depend solely upon your income.

Debt Management

Establish good credit. Get a credit card, use it, and pay it off every month. You don't have to pay interest to have good credit. You just need to make all of your payments on time. You may have a car loan in addition to your credit card.

Marriage and Partnering

It is likely you will marry or live with a partner during this time. It is very important to establish your personal money goals and your joint goals. Initiate talks about money so you both feel comfortable discussing the subject. You can write a financial plan that works for both of you. Your plan needs to account for the fact that you are two different people with both shared goals and individual goals.

Discuss your shared goals and your individual goals. Once you have agreed on your shared goals, then be very honest in expressing your personal goals. Your financial plan can accommodate both of you. Hopefully, you and your partner will agree on certain basics such as the use of credit cards. You may have different investing styles that need to be considered. Have fun with this. It's a wonderful way to get to know your partner better. It also sets the standard for money discussions between you. Remember there is no right or wrong. People are just different. Your financial plan can accommodate both of your interests and needs.

Ages Thirty-five to Forty-five

During this stage of life, you will probably purchase a home and take on the responsibility of a mortgage. If you already have a home, you may want a larger place to accommodate your growing family.

Insurance Needs

If you have children or other dependents, you will need life insurance in addition to health and disability insurance. I believe you should buy insurance to insulate yourself from financial risk. Don't be talked into buying life insurance as an investment. There are numerous ways to structure life insurance, so find someone who will explain the alternatives open and who will help you make well-informed, financially sound decisions. Buy life insurance from a highly rated insurance company. You want the company to be in business if you have to make a claim. Ask the agent to see the solvency ratings of the insurance company you are considering. Or you can call your state's insurance division to check on any insurance company that does business in your state. Don't buy an insurance policy if you don't understand it. If your insurance agent can't explain a policy in terms you can understand, find another agent. Shop around before you buy and know what you are buying.

Employee Benefits

Get copies of your company benefits from your employer. Study the booklet so you know what you have. If you have life insurance, find out how much it will pay if you die. Ask if you can purchase additional insurance through your employer plan. Group plans are often less expensive than individual plans. The drawback is that you might not be able to convert your group policy to an individual policy when you leave. Furthermore, if you have to go into the marketplace for life insurance later in life, you might not be insurable for some reason.

If you depend upon your salary to live, think about purchasing disability insurance if you are not covered through your employer. Disability insurance pays a monthly benefit if you become disabled and cannot work. The benefits can be complicated, and they vary from policy to policy. Before you buy disability insurance, educate yourself about the different types of plans, their benefits, and costs.

Do not cash out your retirement plan if you decide to leave your job. Put the assets into a rollover IRA and keep them growing. Note: If you leave the job market for any length of time, try to keep your skills intact so you will be prepared when and if you decide to rejoin the workforce.

Estate Planning

By the time you are in your forties, your net worth is very likely growing. This is a good time to discuss your estate planning issues with an estate planning attorney. You will want to execute a Will so you can choose where your assets will go when you die. If you have minor children, it is imperative for you to have a Will so that you can name a guardian. This will protect your children if both you and your husband or partner die.

If you die intestate (without a Will), you cannot choose how your things will be divided. The court in your state will do it for you. Verbal and handwritten declarations do not hold up in court. Make sure your Will is properly written, witnessed, and executed. Give a copy to someone you trust to make sure your Will is honored. Execute a Will when you are younger, if circumstances warrant one.

Elderly Parents

If you have elderly parents, you can discuss their estate planning issues with them if they are willing. As an adult child, you may want to know what will happen upon your parents' death and what they would like to have happen. If they have a large estate, there are many strategies they can use to minimize the tax impact. You can also talk with your parents about purchasing long-term care insurance. The biggest financial challenge your parents face may be using up all of their money and more if they become ill. Even if they are younger than age fifty, it's a good time to start this conversation. Hopefully, you and your parents can discuss money issues without too much emotion. However, if you don't have this sort of relationship, there isn't much you can do. Their money is their money. They have the right and the freedom to use it any way they wish.

Investing

It is important during this "accumulation phase" of your life that you continue to invest rather aggressively. It would be great if you have enough money to invest in a regular taxable portfolio. If you pay taxes on your investment income every year, you can use the money any time you want without paying an IRS penalty. The money you invest through your retirement plans can't be used without penalty until you are age fifty-nine and a half. This is rather restrictive. Your taxable portfolio is always available to you because you pay the taxes as you go. I'm sure you have friends who have had to use their 401(k) money because they had an emergency. If you have savings and taxable investments, you can allow your retirement accounts to grow for your future when you want them.

At this stage, you are right on target if you have three types of accounts for your future.

1. Get in the habit of having adequate savings.

2. Contribute to retirement plans, both at work and through an IRA.

3. Put money into a taxable investment portfolio you can use any time you want.

Ages Forty-five to Fifty-five

Women this age are often called the "sandwich generation." That's because they are right in the middle of taking care of their aging parents and putting their children through college. Furthermore, if you had your children later in life, you may be facing retirement and children's college costs at the same time. This won't be a problem if you have been planning for this time and putting money away for twenty or more years.

Investing

If you have not been diligent about investing your money, now is the time to vigorously add to your retirement plans and to your taxable investment portfolio. You have many years to put your money to work for you, so there is still time. You may want to take on an extra job and put all of the proceeds into your investments. Continue to invest for growth. You can be a bit less aggressive in choosing your investments. For example, if you were primarily invested in aggressive growth sectors of the economy, now is the time to pull back a bit and invest in index funds or larger company stocks. Portfolio diversification is important, at all stages of life.

Insurance Needs

You might begin looking into long-term care insurance for yourself during this decade. The younger you are, the cheaper it is. Of course, you might have to pay the premiums for years before you need the insurance. This is clearly a judgment call. Determine whether you still need life insurance and disability insurance. If you do, determine how much longer you will need to carry these forms of insurance.

College for Children

Many women who raise children alone just don't have the money to put into a college savings fund. If you are in this situation, look into scholarships and financial aid. If they are not available, student loans may be the only answer. If you have extra money, help your children with college. If not, they are on their own. Don't jeopardize your financial future to pay for your child's education. Your children can reduce their college expenses by attending a less expensive school, or by attending school part-time and holding down a part-time job. This may not be what either you or your child wants, but it may be better than the alternative, which is incurring huge student loans that are difficult to repay or not going to college at all.

Ages Fifty-five to Sixty-five

Women in this age range are on the cusp of retirement—maybe. However, you may not feel at all ready to retire at the age of sixty-five. You just might want to change direction and do something completely different. I believe that "retirement" as we customarily think about it is not a very useful concept because it focuses on what we are leaving (work) rather than on what we are moving toward (a different lifestyle).

When you are retired, you no longer need to work for money. You now have the choice about how you use your time. You may want to work for money or you may not. It's your choice. You have this choice if you have put your money to work over the years. You have worked and made money and the money you invested has worked and made money. When your money has made enough money, you can stop. Isn't that great? This can be a glorious time in your life. You may want to put aside money for your grandchildren's college expenses. Or you might want to help your children purchase a home. You are entering a stage of life that is filled with grace and tranquility, providing you have taken care of yourself and your money throughout the years. But don't give money away that you may need later on. Be careful with your generosity.

Insurance Needs

You can most likely give up your disability and life insurance policies, if you still have them. You may already have dropped your life insurance as your net worth increased and your children left the nest. However, if you are still working and still need your income, keep your disability insurance. If not, drop it. It stops at age sixty-five.

Health insurance is very important as you age. As you approach the age when you can get Medicare benefits, shop for Medigap health insurance to supplement your benefits. If you don't have long-term care insurance, add that to your list. If you are married, make sure you have long-term care insurance for your husband. It is statistically very likely that you will outlive your husband. Many widows are poor because they spent the family money taking care of their husband during his final illness. Long-term care insurance for your aging husband may be even more important than insurance for yourself.

Investing

Invest your money for growth and income. Up until retirement, you have been investing for growth. Now that you need to live on your investments, you need to invest accordingly. You are going to live a long time, so don't take all of your money out of the stock market. Hire a financial advisor to help you figure out what you need and how to manage your portfolio accordingly.

Over Age Sixty-five

You are in the prime of your life. Women in their seventies and eighties are out climbing mountains, attending yoga retreats, and enjoying life in ways rarely seen before. Continue to make the most of your money just as you have been doing throughout the years. Your financial plan doesn't change much from decade to decade. You need to just tweak it here and there.

Managing Money During Retirement

- Make sure you know what your monthly expenses are.

- Keep enough money in your savings account for emergencies, travel, taxes, and other expenses. You can determine every year how much you want in your savings account.

- Keep your health insurance and your long-term care insurance policies current.

- Invest with both growth and income in mind.

Put five years worth of your income needs into fixed-income investments. This is a good idea because you don't want money that you need to pay your bills invested in the stock market. Here's how to break it up: Keep six months of your expenses in a money market account so you always have the cash you need. Put four and a half years' worth of your expenses into fixed-income investments such as different types of bond funds. Set aside money to pay your taxes as well; you can keep the tax money in a money market fund along with your six months' worth of expenses.

Invest the rest of your portfolio in growth stocks or mutual funds that invest in growth stocks.

Here's an example of how it works.

Suppose you have $500,000 invested and you need $2,000 a month to meet your expenses. You invest accordingly:

$12,000	Money market account or cash account (*six months' expenses*)
<u>$108,000</u>	Fixed-income mutual funds (*four and a half years' expenses*)
$120,000	Available for your cash needs for five years (for the near term)
$500,000	Amount you have to invest
($120,000)	Available for your cash needs for five years (for the near term)
$380,000	Growth stocks and mutual funds (for the long term)

If you don't put some of your money into growth investments, you are in danger of outliving your money. I've seen women who put all of their money into savings accounts and then found it very difficult to meet their expenses as the years passed.

It is unlikely you will outlive your money if you don't take more than six percent out of your portfolio every year. Ibbotson Associates calculated historical stock performance and arrived at these numbers: Since 1961, small company stocks have returned 14 percent on average, while large company stocks returned 10 percent. If you take only six percent to live on, you will have a cushion both for inflation and lower market returns.

Figure Out If You Have Enough to Retire

It is an excellent idea to have enough money to retire before you retire. You don't want to quit your job and find out in twenty years that you no longer have enough money to meet your expenses. Here is how you can figure it out: If you want to stop working, you absolutely need to know your monthly expenses and the amount you will need for taxes. If you know you need $2,000 a month including taxes, you can retire with $400,000 ($400,000 multiplied by .06 equals $24,000 or $2,000/month). This does not include taxes. If your expenses before taxes are $2,000/month, you need to have $2,500 in a twenty-five percent tax bracket ($2,000 multiplied by 1.25 equals $2,500).

If you need $5,000 a month before taxes, you will need to have $1 million working for you ($1,000,000 multiplied by .06 equals $60,000 or $5,000/month). If you pay taxes at twenty eight percent, you will have $3,600 left ($5,000 multiplied by .72 [which is your tax rate subtracted from 100] equals $3,600.) This means that a million-dollar portfolio generates income of between $3,000 and $4,000 after taxes. This may surprise you. Many people believe millionaires live on easy street. Actually it generates only a modest income for life.

As you get older, you can spend a larger percentage of your portfolio. Very likely it will continue to grow even though you are taking money from it so there will be more money. Also, you have fewer years of life left when you will need the money. Be sure to set up a mechanism for moving the cash from your portfolio into your checking account. You can have it deposited automatically every month or every quarter. Or you can write yourself a check from your investment account and deposit it into your checking account. There may be other options available. The point is that your peace of mind demands that you have access to your money without having to calling a broker or someone else to ask for it.

If you have been faithfully putting money away all of your life, now is the time to enjoy it. There is nothing wrong with spending principal from time to time. If you want to take a trip and you don't have the cash, take it from your portfolio without thinking twice. If your portfolio has grown, spend it. However, if the market is in a slump, be more careful. Wait for the market to pick up again. You can be as creative as you want at this stage of your life. Enjoy your free time. Use your money wisely while having fun.

Don't Forget Taxes

Your financial plan at every stage of life needs to include taxes. Taxes are a part of life that cannot be ignored. When you are determining how much you need to live on each month, factor in your tax rate. This will tell you how much you need to earn to pay your bills and your taxes. Don't worry about taxes. Sure you should do everything you can to minimize your taxes. But by all means, live the life you want. Don't make decisions based solely on the tax impact. Paying taxes is a consequence of making money. People who don't pay taxes are usually people who don't have money.

The tax code is designed to persuade Americans to behave in a certain manner. For example, the home interest deduction tells us we value owning a home. Before the year 2000, a retired person between sixty-five and seventy had to pay taxes on any Social Security benefits she received if she earned over a certain amount. This tax law was repealed in 2000 in response to the need for more workers, including those over age sixty-five. The tax code can only be understood within the context of human behavior.

 Think About It . . .

Getting clear about taxes is important. Ask yourself the following questions and write the answers in your journal.

- *Do I understand the federal tax system?*

If your answer is "no," find someone who can help educate you. The IRS has various publications that may be of use and there are books at the library that can help you. The tax code is very complicated. Congress changes it all the time. So you don't just learn it once. You have to keep on top of it. One good way to keep up-to-date about taxes is to read the newspapers. They report on changes in the tax code. They also regularly discuss tax issues around April 15. Read the articles.

- *Do I check with a CPA before I make life decisions?*

There is a tax consequence for every life decision you will ever make. Know the consequences before you marry, divorce, quit your job, get a job, have children, or make any other significant life change. You don't want to make a choice based solely upon taxes, but you do want to give yourself the benefit of understanding what impact your choice will have on your taxes prior to tax time.

- *Do I relax and recognize that taxes are just a part of life?*
Try not to turn yourself inside out to avoid paying taxes. Recognize that taxes are a part of life you may not like, but they won't destroy you. Just pay your taxes on time, as you would any other bill that comes due. Try feeling gratitude for living in the United States.

- *Do I get a big tax refund every year?*
You may enjoy getting a tax refund. Many people count on it to pay off certain bills. However, this isn't really a very good idea because you are actually giving the government an interest-free loan during the year. You could have used that money to pay your bills during the year. Check your withholdings to make sure you are not paying too much. You will know you have succeeded when you don't owe any taxes and you don't get money back.

How Much Is Enough?

The ultimate financial question is this: How much money do you need to live the life you choose? Your plan begins with this question. There is a very easy model to use in determining how much is enough. If you know how much is enough you will probably create enough. If the number is specific, you have a concrete goal to work toward. If your goal is vague, you may not ever make it, or you might not recognize it when you do hit your target.

Your challenge is to enjoy today while putting money away so that you can make choices about what you do in the future.

 Think About It . . .

Here is a format for determining how much is enough. This is a numbers exercise. Work through this process to reach actual dollar amounts. Then determine the choices you can make today that will bring you enough money to live your dreams in your future. Start with pencil and paper and then

transfer your plan to a computer later. Ultimately, you will produce a six- to eight-page working document on a word processor.

Your Financial Plan

We will begin by looking inward. The first three sections of your written plan deal with your internal landscape when it comes to money. Your plan is for you alone. No one else could write these sections of your plan but you. If you have a husband or partner, ask them to work with you on a joint plan. Do the first three sections individually and then compare your answers. This will give you a wonderful way to have an unemotional, meaningful dialogue about life and money. You will find out some extremely valuable things about yourself and your partner.

Leave all judgments out of this process. If you get into judgments about where you are or what you want, you may get too bogged down with emotion to finish the plan. This process is intended to assist you in moving forward into the life you want. The only value for looking backward is to determine your starting point.

Your Current Situation

Describe where you are right now. Include your marital status, your age, and the number of children you have, and any other dependents. Write down the type of car you drive. Think about any inheritances or chunks of money you expect to receive. Think about any big expenses you have coming up within the next five years. This includes college expenses, expenses with your house, travel, etc. List your net worth and anything else that will help you understand your current circumstances.

Your Life Dreams and Goals

Make a list describing how you want to live your life. Do you want to retire? At what age? Does your spouse or partner want to retire? Do you want to educate your children? Go back to school? Travel? If you want to travel, ask yourself where you want to go and the number of times in a year. List the big items that are on your pent-up demand list. Think of anything and everything that would make you feel happy, both now and as you look into the future.

Eventually, you will need to put a dollar amount to the items on your pent-up demand list. Then you can decide when you will have the money to pay for them.

Your Challenges

Think about the obstacles and challenges that could prevent you from meeting your life goals. Perhaps you lack the money or the education. You could be challenged by your past behaviors and attitudes about money. Review the beginning of this book and identify any psychological or emotional obstacles you face. One very common obstacle is not having a clear vision and/or a written plan to achieve your vision.

You can prepare the rest of the following sections without any emotional investment at all. These sections will merely assist you in figuring out where you are financially. If you are in a painful place about your money, try to pretend you are looking at someone else's finances. This may help you move through it quickly, without emotion. You can't do anything about the past except to understand it. Once you understand it, you can move forward into the future you want.

Your Assets

Before you begin listing assets, take note of any insurance policies you have. Hopefully, you buy term insurance so you can list the benefit amount, the monthly payment, and the beneficiary. If you purchase whole life or another type of policy that builds up a cash value, list the cash value under your financial assets. Also, make a note about your estate planning. Do you have a current Will? If you have significant wealth, do you have your estate protected from taxes by using other methods that are currently available? These aren't assets, they are in place to protect your assets.

Now, list of all your financial assets. There is no right order in which to list your assets. I use the following order because it makes sense to me. You can use whatever makes sense to you. Just make sure you have all the information written down so you can see what there is and how it needs to be managed.

Real Estate

Begin with any *real estate* you own such as your home, rental properties, vacant land, time shares, etc. List the purchase date, purchase price, market value today, mortgage amount and terms. Include interest rate/number of years, payment, property taxes. Figure out the equity you have in each property by subtracting the mortgage amount from today's market value. If you own real estate with someone else, write down how it is held. Real estate can be held as tenants in common, tenants in the entirety (for married couples only) or as joint tenants with rights of survivorship.

Financial Assets

Next, list your financial assets. *Liquid assets* include money in checking or savings accounts, money markets, Treasury bills, or CDs. This is money you can get your hands on quickly. List how the money is held—jointly with your spouse/partner or anyone else or individually in your name alone. Add it up.

Next, list everything you have already put away for *retirement.* This is money that is growing tax-deferred or tax-free, in the case of a Roth IRA. Your individual retirement accounts (IRAs), any tax sheltered annuities (TSAs), 403(b) or 401(k) balances, profit sharing plans, and any other plans. List them individually by account. Include how they are currently invested and the total dollar amount. Add it up. (Note: All retirement assets are held in a trust in one person's name only. You cannot have joint retirement accounts.)

Now, list your *taxable investment accounts.* This includes the investment portfolios you have created with money put away after-tax. You pay taxes on income into these accounts every year. You can use these funds for any purpose at any age. Again, list them individually by account, investment, and dollar amount. Add it up. (You can hold these assets individually or jointly, so make a note of how the assets are held.)

List your possessions that have a stable market value such as art, jewelry, and a grand piano under a category of *other assets.* Leave your household items off the list. You get only garage sale value for them, and they aren't worth your effort. Most things lose their market value dramatically the minute you purchase them.

Debt

List all of your creditors, the balance due, terms of payment, percentage rate, etc. Include the list you made in chapter 7.

Net Worth

Write your *net worth* as a line item under your current situation. Your net worth is equal to your assets minus your debts. Do the math. (If you have $175,000 in assets and $65,000 in debts or liabilities, your net worth is $110,000.) If your net worth is a negative number, don't worry, you are on your way toward changing that just by getting this far.

Income

List your annual income. Include salaries, Social Security benefits, other pensions and payments, rental income, spousal/child support, etc. (Determine your take-home pay by multiplying your net check by the number of checks you receive in a year. Then divide that number by twelve. If you are paid every other week, you receive twenty-six paychecks. If you are paid twice a month, you receive twenty-four paychecks.) This makes a difference. If you aren't paid a salary, state your income as realistically as possible. By the way, getting paid erratically makes it more difficult to manage money, so you need to keep very good records of your income and expenses. You will want to have at least six months of your expenses in a savings account so you will always have a cushion. Don't be lulled into supplementing your income with credit card debt.

Don't include your investment income here. If you live on your investment income, you can figure that out later on.

Next, determine the taxes you pay on the rest of your income. Deduct all of your taxes from your gross income. This will tell you the amount of money you have every month.

Expenses

Now, go through all of your expenses and list them in categories. (You may already have done this if you have completed chapter 7.) Don't skip over any of your expenses. You can't know how much is enough unless you know how much money you spend or want to spend.

Subtract your expenses from your income. You might be surprised to see how close or how far apart the figures are. Make a note of any shortfall so you know what you are aiming for. You only have income and expenses to work with. One client laughed when I told her she didn't overspend, she under-earned. This may be your situation. You may be spending more than you create because you don't create enough.

If you have inherited money and live on your investment income, this plan works as well as it does if you live on a salary. Or perhaps you supplement shortfalls with investment income. If you live on investments, make sure you don't spend more than six percent of the principal unless you are over the age of seventy unless you have significant wealth. If you currently spend more than that, adjust either your income or your expenses. Don't put yourself in danger of running out of money.

Managing Your Cash Flow

You can manage your cash flow very easily by making a list of the cut-off dates of your credit cards, cell phone bill, etc. If you are in danger of using too many minutes on your cell phone, for example, quit using it until a new billing cycle has started. Check with your provider to see how many minutes are left until your next billing cycle. The free minutes are great, the extra minutes are usually very expensive. It pays to stay within the minutes provided by your program. Do the same thing with your credit cards. Tally up your expenses and quit using your credit card until a new billing cycle has begun. My VISA card cycle runs from the 11th to the 10th of each month. I quit using it until the 11th if I am in danger of having a bigger bill than I want. You can only do this with discretionary purchases. You must pay your utilities when due. It would be difficult to go without water while waiting for a new billing cycle.

Questions

Ask yourself what you need to know that you don't know already. Do you need to know your tax bracket? Do you need to have your Will and estate plan updated? Do you need less insurance? Do you need to know more about your 401(k) plan? Do you need to know how much something on your pent-up demand list costs?

Observations

Write down your observations about where you are right now as a result of the choices you have made. Do you have too much debt? Do you need to reduce your expenses or increase your income? Do you need to put more money into investments?

Set Your Intentions

The final sections of your plan are important. What are you going to do now—today—to achieve your dreams and goals? Write your intentions in the first person. "I am going to get a part-time job and put all the money I make into investments." "I am going to contribute $100 more every month to my 401(k)." "I am going to be debt-free by _____ (name the month and year)." "I am going to spend my money more freely and not worry so much about it." Your written intention sets you firmly on the path to success.

Action Steps

Once you have written your intentions, list the action steps you are going to take to achieve your dreams. Be very specific. If you are going to reduce your spending, write down how much each month, and in what category. If you are going to get a better job, write down exactly how you are going to go about getting it, how much you will be paid, and when. If you are going to educate yourself more about money, write down how you can do that.

You can use this process to plan your entire financial future or for a specific financial purpose. All financial plans begin with what you want. For example, if you are trying to determine how much you need to retire, go through the steps with that in mind. Once you know what your monthly expenses will be when you retire, you can figure out how much money you will need to have invested to generate that much income. If you want to put money away for your kids' college educations, again, determine how much you will need and go from there.

If you are saving money for a car, you need to know how much the car costs so you will know how much you have to put away. If you want to travel, you need to know where and how much it will cost. Naturally, it costs more to travel around the world on a cruise ship than it does to travel around the United States in a recreational vehicle.

Determining how much is enough may seem like an arduous process. But it is worth doing. I believe it is your key to financial success. You can create a magical, wonderful life if you work with clarity and intention, real numbers, and create a plan for purposeful action. It is never too early and it is never too late.

Chapter Nine

Investing: How Does Your Money Grow?

Money is a very excellent servant, but a terrible master.

P. T. Barnum (1810–1891)

Investing is not something to take lightly; your investment choices are critical to your future well-being. If you invest well, you can secure a solid future for yourself. If you don't make good choices, you may find you don't have the money you need to enjoy life as you get older. Think of investing as putting your money to work. Your money makes money. If you put your money to work thoughtfully and carefully, it will grow over time. This is the reason you invest—so your money can make more money.

This chapter is dedicated to those of you who are new to investing. It explains how the market works and offers basic information about the world of finance and investing. The information presented here is very elementary, very general in nature, and is not intended to be a complete investment guide. There are many exceptions and nuances to managing an investment portfolio that may not be mentioned here. This chapter is intended only to give you a foundation for future learning. Note that real estate is not a financial investment. It represents another asset class altogether and it is not discussed in this chapter.

The world of finance has its vocabulary just as any industry does. If you want to become a savvy investor, it is essential to master the language of investing. It is not difficult. No one learned Finance as her first language and no one was born knowing how to invest. Everyone who wants to invest has to learn how. The language may seem daunting at first, but others have learned it and so can you.

 Think About It . . .

Take a look at the Language of Investing at the back of this book before you continue reading this chapter. Look through all of the terms and read the definitions just to acquaint yourself with them, but don't try to memorize their meaning. After you have looked at it for a while, come back to this chapter and resume reading. Whenever you come across an unfamiliar term, look it up. When you read an unfamiliar word in its context and then look it up, you will understand its meaning better. Don't be intimidated if you have to look up a word or phrase several times. You are learning a new language and this is how it's done.

Saving and Investing

There is a big difference between saving and investing. *Saving* means to save money for use within the next five years. It is for the short term. Investing is for your future. It is for the long term.

Saving Your Money

If you will need your money within the next five years, save it, don't invest it. When you save money, you are saying to yourself, "I want my money back." For example, if you save $100, you will very likely get your $100 back even when you consider the effects of taxes and inflation on that money. If you are receiving interest on your money, basically you are saving it. You are paid interest with a savings account kept at a bank or a credit union. You can also have your savings in a bank money market account or in a mutual fund money market fund. Mutual fund money market funds pay higher rates of interest because they are not protected by the federal government through the FDIC.

Certificates of deposit (CDs) also generate interest, but they lock up your money for a certain period of time, which means that you do not have access to it until the term of the agreement is over. The longer your money is not available, the higher the interest rate you will receive for it.

Bonds or Fixed-Income Securities

If you will need access to your money within the next three to five years, you could consider putting it in bonds. You can buy bonds from the U.S. Treasury, state and local governments and agencies, and companies. Think of a bond as a transition investment between saving and investing. With a bond, you loan your money for a certain period of time at a specific rate of interest. This is why bonds are called fixed-income investments. The interest paid on the bond doesn't change. The price of bonds goes up and down with interest rates, so in addition to earning interest you also can make money on bonds if the price goes up and you sell before they reach maturity. You buy a bond primarily, though, so that you can have the interest income. Any capital gain with bonds is a bonus.

Many people believe their money is less at risk when it is invested in bonds or bond mutual funds. This may not be true. Jeremy Siegel (1994) states that "The safest long-term investment has clearly been stocks, not bonds. For horizons of twenty years or more, bonds are riskier than stocks." He further states, "In the long run, the true risk resides with fixed-income investments, not with common stocks."

Investing Your Money

If you have more than five years before you will need your money, you can invest it. When you invest, you are saying to yourself, "I want my money to make more money." This is very different than saying you want your money back. You don't want only your money back. You want *more* than your money back. You want your $100 to become $200, which it will do in seven years at 10 percent.

When you invest money, you own something. When you own something and it increases in value, you can sell it for more than you paid for it. This is how your money makes money. You can make money by owning two basic types of assets: real estate and stocks. (Note that there are other types of investments, such as precious metals and commodities. However, our discussion is confined to owning stocks. If you want to invest in ownership of other assets make sure you understand what you are buying, how you make money, and the time frame for the investment. Also, determine the amount of risk you are taking.) Of course, if you own something and it loses value, you lose money if you sell it. This is the risk. You don't want to have to sell if your investments have lost money. This is why you invest money you won't need for five years. When you have ownership, you don't get interest. You get capital gains. If you invested $100 in a stock and it grew in value to $200, your capital gain would be $100. In addition, with stock ownership, you may also receive dividends if the company you own decides to divide some of its profits with its owners, the stockholders (or shareholders).

One big difference between saving and investing is that you receive the interest on your savings without having to do anything for it. The interest payments just appear on your statement as the institution's payment for the use of your money.

With stocks, however, you usually don't make money until you sell them. And, you get income, not interest. Income consists of dividends and capital gains. You receive dividends while you own a stock, but you don't get capital gains until you sell your stock. You don't actually make or lose money until you sell your shares of a company. Any increase or decrease happens only on paper since you haven't yet realized the gain or loss. This is called "paper profits" or "paper losses."

Jeremy J. Siegel traced the value of a dollar invested in various asset classes from 1802 to 1992 (1994). Stocks overwhelmingly outperformed every other financial investment. He calculated the following total real return, which is the return adjusted for inflation.

Stocks	$1 grew to $260,000
Bonds	$1 grew to $563
Treasury bills (cash)	$1 grew to $250
Gold	$1 grew to $1.14

Note that the price of gold or real property doesn't compound. The price is the price. Financial assets *compound* over time so you get a return on your return. For example, if you invest $100 and it grows by 10 percent the first year, you will have $110. If it gains 10 percent the next year you have $121, which includes the increase in value of the first year plus the second year. In the figures quoted above, inflation decreased the purchasing power of the dollar from one dollar in 1802 to nine cents in 1992. The figures speak for themselves.

Learn About the Stock Market

The best way to learn about the stock market is to set an intention to be a successful investor. If you decide you want to invest successfully, you will want to get all of the information you need to know to succeed. When I started learning about investing, I had a difficult time reading books about it. I found I did very well by just reading a few newspapers every day. The newspaper defines any concept it mentions right in the article. If you pay attention and read for understanding and learning, you can do it easily. Just decide to read the business section of a newspaper as a daily habit.

At the moment, you may think investing is boring. You don't want to listen to the financial news or to read the business section of the newspaper. However, when you understand the language of investing, you may find it fascinating. Business is not about buildings, money, capital gains, or losses. Business is primarily about people. By listening to the financial news or reading the business section, you will learn to know companies intimately: their leadership, markets, struggles, and triumphs. Moreover, if you have money invested in a company, you will care about its performance and any news about the company will be guaranteed not to bore you.

The Stock Market

The term "stock market" conjures up all sorts of ideas. Some women describe it as gambling, others as motion, "It's always going up and down." Some people think "stock market" and "risk" are synonyms. However, in truth, *the stock market is companies.* That's all it is. There are probably about 10,000 American companies that you can own. These companies are publicly held, which means that they are owned by the general public. The Securities and Exchange Commission (SEC) has many rules and regulations that publicly held companies must observe. For example, a publicly held company has to hold annual shareholder meetings, they must have audited financial statements, and they must send an annual report to their shareholders. A stock certificate represents ownership in a publicly held company. Note that stocks are also called equities because you have ownership. It is just like the equity in your home. The equity is the amount you own.

Publicly Held vs. Privately Held Companies

Most companies are not publicly held, they are privately held. This means that a few people, who either started the company or invested in it, own it. Shares of a privately held company are not available for sale to the public. Most of the companies you see in your neighborhood and town are privately held. For example, a few people may get together to start a restaurant, a dry cleaners, or a manufacturing or service business. These people then own all of the stock in the business.

Most publicly held companies began as privately held companies. You see large, publicly held companies spinning off divisions or product lines into different publicly held companies. AT&T has done this several times. You also see publicly held companies bought by other companies, so they are not publicly held anymore. One example would be IBM's purchase of Lotus, or the purchase of United Airlines by its employees.

The Initial Public Offering

The executives of a privately held company may decide they want to "go public." This will mean they will no longer hold all of the shares. To that end, they announce an initial public offering (IPO). This means that the public is invited to purchase and own shares in their company. Their motivation for the change in the company's status is one or all of the following reasons:

1. They want to get more money so their company can grow. They may have a great small business that they believe can grow into a huge, international organization. But they don't have the money to hire the people, design the products, and get their goods into the marketplace. The money they get from the IPO provides them with the funds they need to accomplish their long-term goals.

2. They may want money for a variety of other reasons, for example, they might want to pay off debt.

3. They want to know the true value of their shares in the company. As long as a company is privately held, it is difficult to put a price on a share's value. When it is publicly held, the share price is announced with the initial public offering, and as the price changes in trading activity, it can be quantified.

4. The entrepreneurs want to become wealthy. Their shares are worth money in the marketplace. They exchange their privately held shares for publicly held shares. One entrepreneur traded privately held shares he purchased for fourteen cents into publicly held shares at $48. This is an example of money making money!

Once the company has gone public, its stock is held by millions of shareholders, also known as stockholders. (These two terms mean the same thing.) The company gets the money from the new shareholders and the officers of the firm can use the money for its intended purpose. Once a company goes public, it operates under the scrutiny of the Security and Exchange Commission (SEC) regulations. The stock trades on a stock exchange such as the New York Stock Exchange or NASDAQ. The stock exchanges compete for companies to list.

The only time a company receives money when its shares trade is at the IPO, unless the company makes a secondary offering. Once the company is publicly held, its shares trade on the open market. The person who sells shares is the one who receives the money. The company doesn't get the money. The person buying shares pays the person selling shares. The exchanges are there to make sure that the stock trades are in accord with all regulations and procedures.

Managing Your Stock Portfolio

Your portfolio consists of your stocks, mutual funds, bonds, and any cash you have. Any time you have more than one holding as an investment, it is called a portfolio. For example, if you have more than one real estate investment, you would call it your real estate portfolio.

Trading Stocks

You can trade shares of stocks in various places. The SEC monitors the trading activities in the United States. They want to assure investors of an orderly marketplace. Investor confidence is crucial to the entire economy. The stock exchanges have changed dramatically because of the Internet and the ability to trade stocks around the world twenty-four hours a day. As we enter the twenty-first century, the stock exchanges are changing dramatically. This is in response to market forces, international trading, and improved communication and technology.

Newspapers list the stock quotes grouped by where the stock trades. When you open the financial pages, you will notice that all the NYSE stocks are listed under NYSE, for example. Stocks are not listed in the newspaper by their trading symbol. They are listed alphabetically by name in abbreviated form. The trading symbol is used on the tape display and when making trades.

The New York Stock Exchange

The New York Stock Exchange (NYSE), founded in 1792, is the best-known stock exchange in the world. It has traditionally been the place the bigger companies trade. Many people are involved in making the trades on the NYSE in what is called an "auction" market. There is order among the apparent chaos. A specialist who has authority to trade stocks of a certain company, such as Procter and Gamble, is the auctioneer of all trades for that company. Brokers and traders try to get the best deals for their own accounts or for their client accounts. The brokerage firms, such as Merrill Lynch and Salomon Smith Barney, are members of the NYSE. They buy a "seat" on the exchange that gives them the right to trade stocks for their clients. There are 1366 seats or members of the NYSE.

NASDAQ

Many companies, large and small, trade on NASDAQ. Stock trades are made by matching sell orders to buy orders by computers. This used to be called the over-the-counter market (OTC). Many companies like to be listed on NASDAQ because they prefer the system of multiple trading through more than one dealer, rather than by a specialist trading as on the NYSE. NASDAQ stands for National Association of Securities Dealers Automated Quotation system. It is operated under the National Association of Securities Dealers (NASD). There are other exchanges across the country as well, but the NYSE and NASDAQ are the two main places that stocks trade. The American Stock Exchange (AMEX) merged with NASDAQ, but is still a stand-alone exchange, much like the NYSE. It is also located on Wall Street.

Stock Trading Costs

You pay a transaction fee either to buy or sell a stock. The amount you pay depends on where you make the trade. Full-service brokers, such as Paine Webber or Morgan Stanley Dean Witter, offer investment advice with your trades. They charge more than a discount broker, such as Charles Schwab. Discount brokers make your trades without giving you investment advice. You can also trade with an online broker such as E-trade or Ameritrade. Typically, online trading has the lowest transaction costs, but once again, you get no investment advice.

Holding Your Stock Certificates

A stock certificate represents ownership. In the past, you may have been issued stock certificates that you kept in a drawer or in a safe deposit box. But today, stock certificates have pretty much been replaced through the magic of computers. Today, when you buy stocks, it is likely that you buy them through a broker. You open an investment account (called a custodian account because the broker has custody of your assets). Firms, such as Merrill Lynch, E-trade, or a bank act as custodians of your securities. (Remember, both stocks and bonds are commonly referred to as securities.) When you call your broker to buy or sell a stock, you don't actually receive or deliver any stock certificates. Your shares are held in a custodian account at your brokerage firm. The account has your name on it and no one can touch your securities without your permission. You receive a regular statement from your custodian listing the market value of your portfolio, all of the transactions that occurred in your account during the period, the cost basis of your stock (what you paid for it), and other relevant information.

Diversify, Diversify, Diversify

You can reduce the overall risk of your investments by owning many companies in a variety of industries. This is called *diversification*. When you are putting your portfolio together, make sure you diversify your holdings. It makes sense when you think about it. The more variety you have, the less risk you incur. If you own only one or two companies or several companies in the same industry, the individual company or the sector could be devastated in a downturn. If you own shares in only one company for some reason, perhaps you inherited them or you've had them for years, sell some of your shares and diversify. As your stocks grow in value, keep diversifying so you don't have too much in any single company.

Types of Companies to Own

When deciding which stocks to buy, you want to look at the size of the companies that are available to you. There are three basic sizes of companies to own—small, mid-size, and large. This is true if you are invested outside the U.S. in international stocks or even within industries or sectors of the American economy.

Small Company Stocks (Small Cap)

Small cap companies are often called aggressive growth stocks. They are companies that are relatively small, volatile, and entrepreneurial. They try to fill a market niche. They may or may not make it in the competitive world. These companies can be highly volatile. NASDAQ is the place many smaller companies trade. Investors who bought a company when it was small and *stayed in* made a lot of money if the company succeeded. Small company investors make their money by receiving capital gains because small companies do not pay dividends. Small companies put their profits back into the company to make the company grow. Of course, small caps are riskier because thousands of small companies go out of business. A recent good example would be Boston Chicken, which has 77 million shares outstanding and stopped trading in 1999. If you want to invest in small companies, you might do better by buying shares of a mutual fund that invests in them. Small cap mutual funds make it easy for you to diversify your risk. There are thousands of small cap mutual funds. Do your research and use a financial advisor to help you.

Don't be tempted to buy "penny stocks." Those are stocks that sell for less than $1 a share. They are very volatile, speculative investments. They usually trade on regional exchanges. These stocks do not belong in a well-planned, long-term investment portfolio. You want to be very careful about buying a company whose shares are offered for less than $5 unless it is a big company having difficulties, such as Chrysler in the early 1980s.

Growth Stocks (Mid-Cap or Medium-Cap)

Mid-cap companies usually have an aggressive management team with a product or service in a rapidly growing market. These stocks are considered growth stocks. A mid-size company very likely already has strong revenues (sales) and earnings or profits. Starbucks is a good example of a growth stock. Intel is still considered a growth stock, even though it is large company. Growth companies usually do not pay dividends. If they pay a dividend, it is usually small. You make your money through receiving capital gains when you sell your shares for more than you paid for them.

You can probably do your own research and buy individual growth stocks. Or you can buy growth stocks through mutual funds which will help you diversify.

Blue Chip Stocks (Large Cap or Income Stocks)

Stocks of large, stable companies that have been in business for a long time are called blue chip stocks. They have millions of shares outstanding. You probably know the names and products of these companies. IBM, AT&T, Home Depot, and Coca Cola are good examples of blue chip stocks. You can receive income from blue chips without selling your shares because they pay dividends. Blue chip companies pay dividends because they aren't plowing all of their earnings back into the company to make the company larger. They are already big. Investors believe blue chip companies have more staying power and are less likely to go out of business than smaller companies. Their share price increases but probably not as spectacularly as a small company price might. This is the trade-off for not taking as much risk. You can buy individual blue chip stocks or invest in them by buying a blue chip or large cap growth mutual fund. If a mutual fund is an equity-income fund, it is a large cap.

International Stocks

You can buy shares in companies that are not based in the United States, which may help balance out your portfolio. Interest rates, inflation, unemployment, and other factors that influence a company's success often move in different patterns outside the U.S. You may lower the overall risk and volatility in your portfolio by investing outside the U.S.

There are certain risks that investors in foreign companies need to know about. They include the following:

1. Currency fluctuations

2. The difficulty of getting current and accurate information about a company

3. Trading costs may be more expensive

4. Foreign governments may be unstable, which can negatively affect a company's ability to do business

A sophisticated investor may be able to ferret out good international stocks. The average investor will do better to buy a mutual fund that invests in international stocks. An international fund buys only foreign companies. A global fund or a worldwide fund buys American companies as well. For true international diversification, stick to the international funds.

Stock Splits

Over time small companies become big companies. The number of shares outstanding (owned by the public) grows and grows until many large companies have millions of shares outstanding. The number of shares available to the public is determined by two basic processes:

1. The company issues more shares in secondary offerings. All stock offerings after the IPO are called secondary offerings. Over the years a company can file many secondary offerings with the SEC.

2. A company with a rapidly growing stock price may split its stock. The company can split its stock so that the number of shares doubles, triples, or even quadruples giving investors more shares at a lower price. This effectively cuts the price of an individual share in half.

Here is the rationale behind stock splits. Most investors purchase stock in lots of 100 shares. These are called *round lots*. The more expensive the stock, the more money the investor needs to invest in that stock. When the stock price gets too high for the average investor to afford 100 shares, the company board of directors will call for a stock split. The most common occurrence is a two for one split. If you already own the stock, you get two shares for each share you own. If you have 100 shares, now you have 200 shares after the split. While your number of shares doubles, the stock price is sliced in half. This allows new investors to buy in at half the price.

Here's how it works: Suppose you own 100 shares of Boeing at $100/share. Your holdings total $10,000 after a two for one stock split. If you own 200 shares of Boeing at $50/share, your holdings still equal $10,000. Your position doesn't change, so it doesn't make much difference to you until the stock price goes up again. Now you have twice the number of shares to grow. As the years go by and the company is profitable, the stock again reaches a high price and splits, giving you 400 shares, then 800 shares, and on it goes.

Check out the price of Berkshire Hathaway A and B shares in the newspaper. It trades on the NYSE. Warren Buffet, the investment guru who runs the company, doesn't split the stock. A round lot is ten shares.

Investment Performance Benchmarks

Are stocks up or down? The search for a single number to describe what is happening to the whole market led to the creation of stock indexes. They are also referred to as "performance benchmarks," "the market," or just the "indexes." A variety of indexes exist to provide a benchmark for various types of securities. Companies may be included in more than one index.

The Dow Jones Industrial Average (DJIA)

This is the most frequently quoted index. Its numbers are on the news every night, so when most people think about how the stock market is doing, they are referring to the Dow Jones. When people talk about "the market" they are usually referring to the Dow. The Dow is so popular because it is the oldest index, dating back to 1884. However, the Dow is not a very useful index to measure your portfolio because it includes only thirty companies. The Dow Jones Industrial Average measures the emotion of the market—that is, are people feeling positive (bullish) or negative (bearish). The Dow has been more volatile as technology companies have been added and old industrials have been dropped.

Standard and Poor's 500 Index (S&P 500)

Standard and Poor's is a subsidiary of McGraw Hill. The company tracks 500 of the largest companies; 400 industrial, 40 financial, 20 transportation, and 40 utility. The 500 companies in the S&P 500 are widely held. This means millions of shareholders own shares in these companies. Experts use the S&P 500 as the benchmark for overall market performance.

NASDAQ Index

The NASDAQ index includes nearly 5,000 stocks of smaller companies, which are generally traded over-the-counter. NASDAQ started with a value of 100 in 1971. Many large technology companies, such as Intel and Microsoft trade, on NASDAQ.

The Russell 2000 Index

This is the most commonly used index for smaller companies. There is also the Russell 3000 which is the index for 3000 smaller companies. Frank Russell Trust Company of Tacoma, Washington manages these indexes.

The EAFE Index

This index is designed to measure the investment returns of the developed countries outside of North America. It is the best benchmark for international investments. EAFE stands for Europe, Australasia, Far East. Morgan Stanley Capital International produces the EAFE index along with many other, more specific, international indexes.

Putting Your Money to Work

Investing is easier than it may seem. Your investment plan should be part of your overall financial plan. These suggestions assume you have your savings already in place. If you don't have money in savings, start there, and then invest.

There are four basic factors to think about before you invest. They are as follows:

1. **Whether you need growth, income, or both.** If you need income from your investments, don't invest everything in the stock market. Put six months' worth of your expenses into a money market fund in addition to your savings account. Then put four and a half to five years' worth of expenses in bond mutual funds. You do not want the money you need to pay your mortgage invested in stocks (see chapter 7).

2. **The amount of time you have before you want or need your money back.** Time is your best friend when it comes to

investing. Mark Twain called compound interest the "Eighth Wonder of the World." The more money you have working for you over time, the faster it grows. Even if you start with twenty-five dollars a month, it will grow and grow, if you have the time.

3. **The amount of money you have to invest**. If you are investing a lump sum, you can invest it in a diversified portfolio that includes various size companies. If you are investing a small amount over a longer period of time, start with a growth stock or a mutual fund until your account amounts to a few thousand dollars. Then diversify into large companies, and finally into small companies and international investments. Use mutual funds for the small companies and international investments.

4. **The percentage of your money you want to invest in each type of asset**. If you are investing a lump sum, you can determine the percentages you want in each asset class (small cap, growth, large cap, and international.) This is called asset allocation. This is an important decision. For example, your asset allocation could be 20 percent international, 30 percent small and mid-size companies and 50 percent large companies. You can play around with this until you feel comfortable with the mix. Decide what type of asset allocation you want even if you are investing only a small amount of money.

Creating your investment plan is likely to help you bring your hopes and dreams into reality. Also, if you know how you want to invest, you will know exactly what to do with an unexpected bonus or gift of money.

Risk and Stocks

The stock market itself isn't an inherently risky place to put your money. Some companies carry more risk than other companies. Generally, the smaller the company, the greater the risk. This makes sense. Smaller companies are more likely to go out of business than bigger companies. They don't have the means to weather an economic downturn or a marketing disaster.

A well-planned investment portfolio helps to reduce the risk of investing. If you are well diversified, it is unlikely you will lose everything. That's not really your biggest risk anyway. The biggest risk is to take no risk. When you take no risk, you trade today's fears for tomorrow's possibilities. Your biggest financial risk is that you will not have enough money to live your life the way you would like to when you can't work anymore—or if you just don't want to work anymore.

At Tax Time

Every January your custodian, such as Schwab or E-trade, will send you a 1099 form for all of your taxable investments. This lists any dividend income and capital gains or capital losses (profits and losses from sales of stock shares) from the previous year. This information is also reported to the IRS. You need this information to complete your tax return. The federal capital gains tax is either 10 percent or 20 percent for stocks held long term (more than twelve months). (If you are in the 15 percent tax bracket, long-term gains are taxed at 10 percent. It is 20 percent for higher income tax brackets.) Short-term capital gains (for stocks held less than twelve months) are taxed at your ordinary income rate. Dividends and interest are also taxed at your ordinary income tax rate. You might pay state taxes on investment income as well.

Take into consideration the tax implications when you trade stocks. However, try not to let tax factors overwhelm other considerations. Make the wisest choice you can. If it results in a taxable transaction, it's okay. Pay the tax. If you have a well-planned, well-executed investment strategy, you will very likely come out ahead in the long run.

By the way, when you die, the basis (cost) of your investments is "stepped up" to the investments' market value on your date of death. This usually increases the cost basis so your heirs won't have to pay the same tax that you would have paid if you had sold your stocks at a gain. If you have lost money on your investments, this doesn't matter.

The High Cost of Low-Cost Stock

You may pay a high price for not selling a low-cost stock. Low-cost stock is stock you may have held for a long time in a taxable account. You may have bought a stock for $4.50 a share and its price is now $65 a share. If you sell it, you will have a large capital gain and you will have to pay taxes on the gain. If a low-cost stock is the only stock you own, you are certainly at risk because you aren't diversified. If the company goes down the drain, you go with it. If it is not your only stock, but a significantly large holding, you may still want to sell a portion of it to get more diversification.

One strategy for dealing with low-cost stocks in your portfolio is to decide how much you are going to sell every year. One plan would be to sell 20 percent every year until you have sold most of it in five years. You can diversify your holdings with the proceeds, minus the tax. This is a solid investment strategy that will diversify you out of a risky situation. Your low-cost stock may rise forever, but if you never sell it, you never reap the benefits. Keep in mind that all capital gains are tax-deferred. If you want to use the money you put to work for you in the past, eventually, you will have to pay the tax.

A Word About Mutual Funds

A mutual fund is a method of investing; it is not an investment itself. Each mutual fund company is a separate corporation registered with the SEC. Just as Intel is in business to make money by manufacturing computer chips, a mutual fund is in business to make money by investing in various types of investments. You buy shares of the mutual fund just as you would buy shares of Intel. The difference is that a mutual fund holds shares of many companies, not just one. Mutual funds offer an excellent way to diversify your portfolio. Just about any investment that you can buy individually can be bought through a mutual fund.

If you want to put your savings into a mutual fund, you can buy a money market mutual fund where the share price doesn't fluctuate in value. However, bank or credit union savings accounts are guaranteed and mutual funds are not. The FDIC insures bank savings and the National Credit Union Administration (NCUA) insures accounts at credit unions. So you usually will receive more interest from a mutual fund than you would from an ordinary savings account because there are no guarentees.

Advantages of Mutual Funds

I think mutual funds are your best investment choice if you have less than $100,000 to invest. With less than $100,000, you cannot get the appropriate diversification in your portfolio by buying individual stocks. Even if you have more than $100,000, you might still want to invest in mutual funds, particularly if you are buying small cap or international stocks. Mutual funds offer the following benefits:

1. Expert money management.

2. Diversification: there are lots of securities and types of funds.

3. Liquidity: mutual funds are easy to buy and sell.

4. You can easily track performance through the mutual fund companies or from the mutual funds rating services.

5. You can invest a small amount of money.

The Difference Between Load and No-load Funds

Fees, or mutual loads, may or may not be charged when you purchase or sell a fund. A load is also called a sales charge. The load has nothing whatsoever to do with the internal expenses of the fund. All funds have internal expenses associated with managing the fund. Do not confuse the two!

There are two ways to buy mutual funds.

1. No-load funds are sold to you directly by the mutual fund company. There is no broker or financial advisor to give you investment advice. You must make your own investment choices.

2. Load funds are sold to you by a salesperson who is licensed by the NASD to give you investment advice and to sell you mutual funds. You will pay a sales charge or load for getting advice and recommendations from a financial planner, stockbroker, or insurance agent. You can buy load funds at a bank, a brokerage firm, or an insurance agency. Generally, funds carry a front-end load or a back-end load or sales charge. There are a few other categories, but they are rarely used.

   - **Front-end load fund or "A" shares.** With a front-end load, money is deducted from your initial investment. For example, if there is a 4 percent load, a $100 investment becomes a $96 investment. The broker, the company, and others share the $4. Think of it like a real estate commission. Every time you invest in a load fund, a portion is taken out to pay the sales charge. Even though you pay up front, you are better off buying A shares than B shares.

   - **Back-end or deferred load or "B" shares.** With a back-end load, the fund company charges you a fee if you sell your shares before a certain period of time, usually four to five years. If you would get $1,000 when you sell and the deferred load or sales change is 3 percent in the third year, you will get $970 and the investment advisor will get $30.

B shares are designed to prevent you from selling your shares and they have a number of disadvantages. You pay the back-end load on your original investment plus any income or appreciation that accrues. Internal management fees for B shares usually are higher. Often, people are reluctant to sell B shares because it costs money. This keeps them locked in. Basically this makes a liquid investment not liquid. I don't like B shares.

Greed and Fear

The two emotions that move the market are greed and fear. Greed kicks in when the market is going up, as in a bull market. The stock market may be driven to untenable heights because of greed. The more a stock price goes up, the more people jump on the bandwagon and buy it without doing their research. You can see greed at work when stock prices move ahead of a company's ability to earn money for its shareholders in the way of profits.

Fear takes the place of greed when the market goes into a slump or when we experience a bear market. This is when emotional investors dump their stocks and lose their money. Some of these investors vow that they will never buy stocks again. Emotional investing takes a heavy toll on the investor.

The more you know about investing, the less emotional you will be as an investor. Your knowledge and understanding of your investments and of how the stock market works will help you to stay calm no matter what happens. When you invest over time, the volatility of the market won't faze you. It is volatility that creates opportunity. If the stock prices didn't fluctuate, you wouldn't have the returns. Your behavior as an investor is more important for your success than the behavior of the stock market.

Today, the markets are changing because trading is easier than ever. This lures some investors who want to make a quick return. But the stock market is not the place for gamblers or high-stakes players. It is a place for serious investors who are serious about making money over the long term. With a long-term orientation, you don't sell your stocks when their price falls. You may not like it, but you take a deep breath and do absolutely nothing, assuming you are well invested. The money you have invested is money you won't need for five years, so you can relax when stock prices fall for a period of time. If you have more money to invest, you might think of the stock market as just having a sale and buy more shares of stock or mutual funds.

The Habit of Investing

It is the habit of investing that creates wealth. You might be like Emily, a woman I know who told me that previously she always thought only rich people invested. She thought she couldn't ever be rich because she didn't know anyone who was rich. She always felt like she was on the outside looking in. Now she understands it is through investing that people get rich. Anyone can create wealth if they invest wisely over time. The amount of money you invest isn't as important as the fact that you invest at all. Even a small amount of money invested wisely will grow to a tidy sum over time. Here is an example of how it works.

My friend Stephanie got pregnant with her first child in 1957. Her dad was not a wealthy man, but he gave her $125 to invest. Between 1957 and 1993, Stephanie invested $25 at the beginning of each month in a mutual fund where she paid a front-end load of 6 percent. This means she actually invested $23.50 every month for thirty-six years. By 1993, Stephanie had invested a total of $10,277 and her portfolio had grown to $103,000. That year her husband, Phil, decided to retire so she stopped investing, and she started taking $500 a month out of the portfolio. By October of 1999, Stephanie had taken $40,500 from her portfolio. The market value of her investment was $186,673. Today, Stephanie continues to take her $500 a month and her portfolio is still growing.

My friend Helen is another example. Helen became a millionaire at age fifty by putting 10 percent of her money into investments. Helen invested as a habit. Every time she had a little extra money, she bought stocks. Initially, she bought 200 shares of McDonalds. It split and she had 400 shares. It split again and gave her 800 shares. When it split again she owned 1600 shares. Then she had 3200 shares until it split again to give her 6400 shares. McDonalds split again in March 1999. Helen now has a whopping 12,800 shares of McDonalds. This is a good example of how money makes money over time. Helen started small and stayed committed to her investment program.

Managing Your Money Through the Years

As the years go by, continue to invest every chance you get. Your behavior as an investor is more important than the behavior of your investment advisor or the stock market. Don't try to outsmart the market. This is called "market timing" and it typically doesn't work well over the long term. You may guess correctly and pull out your money before the market goes down. But you might not know when to put your money back into the market before it goes up. The best time to invest is when you have the money. Some years you will have losses, but chances are, over a long period of time, your money will make money, if you diversify, work your plan, and stay on track. Watching your portfolio grow over the years will delight you.

Growth stocks will be the major component of your portfolio for most of your life. But when you need money from your taxable portfolio, take it. Leave your retirement funds alone. As you near retirement, you will need income from your portfolio. At that point, over time, start selling some of your stocks and invest in bond mutual funds. Rebalance your portfolio once a year. Look at your cash needs for the coming five years and position your portfolio to meet your needs.

Figure out your net worth every year. Look at your savings and your investments and make sure you are on track. Always keep a savings account for emergencies and opportunities. Use money markets and bond funds for money you will need six months from now and for the next four and a half to five years. Use the same strategy when you start taking money from your retirement accounts.

Get Professional Help

There is much more to learn about investing, but you now have the basics. I caution you against investing on your own unless you are well educated about investing. As in all areas, paying a professional to help you will be money well spent. Now that you know how the market works and you know what you want, you can work very easily with an advisor. If you don't get what you want or if you don't feel comfortable with your advisor, find someone else. Here are a few ideas for selecting an investment advisor:

1. Does the advisor have a good network of referrals?

2. Does the advisor return your calls promptly?

3. Does the advisor listen to you—really listen?

4. Does the advisor handle your money with your specific needs in mind?

5. Does the advisor educate you?

6. Does the advisor make you feel smart and intelligent or somehow lacking?

7. How does the advisor charge?

8. What credentials does the advisor have?

9. How long has the advisor been in business?

10. How many clients has the advisor lost in the past five years and why?

11. Ask to talk with a client reference.

12. Do not be afraid to ask questions and expect answers. Remember it's your money.

Moving Boldly into the Future

Here are a few things to keep in mind as you continue to grow and work with your investments. You will make mistakes, so cut your losses and move on.

1. Figure out what you want and what works for you.

2. Invest in growth assets if you have the time to let your money grow.

3. Diversify your portfolio.

4. Pay attention to what is going on in the marketplace.

5. Read the business section of the newspaper at least three times a week.

6. Know what investments you have and why.

7. Hire a financial advisor to help you.

8. If you do not understand the language your investment advisor uses, find an advisor with whom you can communicate.

Stay on the graceful side of money rather than the greedy side. Manage your money with your head, not your stomach. Enjoy the process of learning and growing. Understand that you are in charge of your life and your money and that you can create the world anyway you choose. Have fun!

THE LANGUAGE OF INVESTING

*Ordinary riches can be stolen, real riches cannot. In your soul
are infinitely precious things that cannot be taken from you.*

Oscar Wilde (1856–1900)

Account Executive. The title given by brokerage firms to their stock-
brokers. Account executives are sometimes also called registered representative, financial counselor, and financial consultant.

Accrued interest. Interest that is due but hasn't yet been paid. Bonds
pay interest every six months, but it is earned (accrued) every month.
If you buy a bond halfway between interest payment dates, you must
pay the seller for the three month's accrued interest. You get the
money back three months later when you receive the interest payment for the entire six months.

American Stock Exchange (AMEX). Located on Wall Street, it
merged with NASDAQ. It is home to many oil and gas companies
and trades shares of foreign companies, too.

Annual meeting. A meeting with management and shareholders that
must be held once a year. Shareholders vote on various issues put
forth by management. If you can't be there in person, you send in a
proxy statement that authorizes someone else to vote your shares the
way you want.

Annual Percentage Rate (APR). The amount of interest you pay calculated on an annual basis.

Annual Percentage Yield (APY). The amount of interest you receive on a CD, or other investment, that pays compound interest.

Annual report. Yearly financial record of a company that, by law, must be distributed annually to all shareholders. It includes a statement of operations, a balance sheet, and an income statement.

Annualized. The annual rate of return. Returns and interest rates are often given for a specific time period, such as a quarter. The annualized rate takes that number and calculates it for a year or a longer period of time. This is true even if you are paying interest.

Annuity. A series of regular payments, usually from an insurance company, guaranteed to continue for a specific time, usually the annuitant's lifetime, in exchange for a single payment or a series of payments to the company. With a deferred annuity, payments begin sometime in the future. A fixed annuity pays a fixed amount for the life of the contract. Variable annuity amounts change depending upon investment results.

Asset. Anything having commercial or exchange value that is owned by a business, institution, or individual.

Asset allocation. The types and percentages of asset classes you invest in to diversify and reduce risk in the portfolio. Asset allocation is also used to reduce portfolio volatility.

Asset class. Each investment type, such as real estate, stocks, bonds, etc., is a separate asset class.

At-the-market. When you buy or sell a security "at-the-market," your broker will execute your trade at the next available price.

Back-end load. A fee charged by mutual funds to investors who sell their shares before owning them for a specified length of time (B shares).

Bearish. A bear thinks the market is going to go down. It is the opposite of "bullish."

Bear market. A prolonged period of falling prices.

Benchmark. The measuring stick used by the finance industry to see how well money managers or mutual funds have performed. They are measured against an index of the same securities that is not managed, such as the Standard & Poor 500 index.

Beta. A measure of price volatility that relates the stock or mutual fund to the market as a whole. A stock or fund with a beta higher than 1 is expected to move up or down more than the market. A beta below 1 indicates a stock or fund that usually moves less than the market.

Bid and asked. "Bid" is the price a buyer is willing to pay; "asked" is the price the seller will take. The difference, known as the "spread," is the broker's share of the transaction. This is how stocks trade on NASDAQ and over-the-counter.

Blue chip stock. A stock with three characteristics: it is issued by a well-known, respected company, has a good record of earnings and dividend payments, and is widely held by investors.

Bond. A bond is an IOU. When you buy a bond, you lend a company (or a government entity) money. You are given a piece of paper (the bond) that states you will be paid back at a certain date and you will be paid interest in the meantime. There are many types of bonds.

Bond rating. Bonds are rated by the issuer's ability to pay the interest and to pay back the loan. Moody's and Standard & Poor's are two of the major bond rating services.

Book value. The book value of the company is determined by subtracting its liabilities from its assets and dividing the sum by the number of shares outstanding. This is a good gauge of a stock's true value.

Bullish. A bull is someone who believes the market is going to go up. The opposite of "bearish."

Capital gain or loss. The difference between what you paid for an investment and what you sold it for.

Capitalization. The total value of a company's long-term debt, capital stock, and surpluses. Also called market cap. Also, the market price multiplied by the number of shares outstanding.

Certificate of deposit (CD). Investments sold by a bank or brokerage house. A CD generally pays a higher rate of interest than a savings account, but there usually is a penalty for taking your money out before the CD matures.

Churning. When a broker generates commissions by buying and selling in your account excessively.

Common stock. You become an owner of the company when you buy its stock. Another name for stock is "equity." As a shareholder, you have the rights of an owner. If the company goes bankrupt, you are paid last. (See preferred stock.)

Compound interest. Interest earned on principal (the original investment) plus the interest earned on the interest. Compound interest grows faster than simple interest. Compound interest refers to interest paid on the money you lend as well as the interest from the previous month or day.

Consumer Price Index (CPI). The measure of changes in consumer prices as determined by a monthly survey of the U.S. Bureau of Labor Statistics. It is the commonly used measure for recording monthly changes in inflation.

Contrarian. An investor who looks for investments that everyone else thinks are duds because they are usually selling at a low price. The contrarian looks for "diamonds in the rough."

Convertible bond. Corporate bonds that can be converted to stock at a certain price.

Coupon. Interest on a bond the issuer promises to pay to the bondholder. A $1000 bond with a 10% coupon rate pays the bondholder $100 in semi-annual payments.

Custodian account. A brokerage, bank, or trust company will hold your securities in an account for you. The securities are issued in the name of the firm (not your name) and held on deposit for you at the depository trust company (DTC). A custodian account is good to have because you don't need to keep track of your own securities; you get a monthly statement of your account activities, and dividends and interest are automatically reinvested in stocks or go into a money market fund.

Day trader. A person who tries to make money by trading the same stock or set of stocks several times during a day. Day traders contribute to market volatility. They are not long-term investors.

Debenture. A corporate bond (IOU) that is not backed by any of the company's assets. Somewhat riskier than a secured bond which is usually secured by real estate or company assets, which are called "collateral."

Default. When a company or institution issues a bond and cannot pay back its investors either the interest or the principal (face value of the bond).

Depository Trust Company (DTC). Located in New York City, it is the central place where stocks and bonds are exchanged. Most of these exchanges take place electronically. The New York Stock Exchange and the major Wall Street brokerage houses own DTC.

Discount broker. A brokerage house that executes your trades for you. They do not give investment advice. They act only on your instructions.

Discretionary account. A brokerage account where you have given your broker or money manager authority to buy and sell without checking with you first.

Diversification. Spreading risk by investing in several categories of investments.

Dividend. A portion of the company's earnings that is paid to the shareholders. Usually dividends are in cash, but sometimes they are paid in the form of additional stock.

Dividend Reinvestment Plan (DRIP). A program where a stockholder can automatically invest the dividends in the company's stock rather than taking cash.

Dollar-cost averaging. Where you invest the same amount of money according to a regular schedule regardless of the price of the stock or mutual fund shares. This allows you to invest systematically and take advantage of volatility.

Due diligence. The investigation and research a broker or mutual fund manager does before investing in a company. The investigation you do before you invest your money.

Earnings per share. A measure of how profitable the company is. It is calculated by taking the after-tax profit, deducting bond interest and preferred stock payments, and dividing that number by the number of shares of common stock outstanding.

Equity. Stocks are referred to as equities because they represent ownership.

Ex-dividend. The period between the time the company declares it is going to pay a dividend and the actual payment of the dividend. On the ex-dividend date, the price of the stock or fund will fall by the amount of the dividend, so new investors don't get the benefit of it. An "X" in the newspaper listings indicates the companies and funds that have gone ex-dividend.

401(k) plan. A company-sponsored retirement plan where the employee is allowed to invest a percentage of salary into the plan rather than take it as cash. Taxes are deferred on that portion of the salary invested in the plan. When the money is taken out of the plan, taxes must be paid on it.

403(b) plan. Similar to a 401(k) plan except it is open only to public employees and employees of not-for-profits. (These titles refer to the specific numbered sections of the IRS code.)

FDIC. The Federal Deposit Insurance Corporation, which insures all bank deposits up to $100,000.

Financial analyst. A person in a brokerage house, bank, or mutual fund company who studies a number of companies and makes buy or sell recommendations on the securities of particular companies and industry groups.

Fixed-income investment. A description of all investments where the amount of the income or interest is known in advance.

Front-end load. The sales commission charged by many mutual fund companies on mutual fund purchases. The load can be from 1% to 8.5%. (Also known as A shares.)

Full-service broker. Full service brokerage firms give investment advice to clients and employ brokers to sell stocks, bonds, and manage accounts that are managed by third-party investment advisors.

Fundamental analysis. A method of evaluating stocks based upon a company's balance sheet, history, management, and product lines and future prospects along with reasonable expectations of the stock's price and dividends. This is the opposite of technical analysis.

Futures contract. A speculative way to make money offered by brokers. You buy a contract or a right to buy something (commodity) at a future time and price. You pay money for the contract and it has a separate value from that of the underlying stock. You need to clearly understand the futures market before you invest because you can lose more than your investment in a heartbeat. You can also make a lot of money, if you have the stomach for it.

Good-till-canceled order. An order placed with a broker to buy or sell a security at a specified price. The order is effective until the stock reaches that price or until you cancel it.

Growth investor. A growth investor is one who believes a company will outperform its previous profits in the future. The price to earnings ratio doesn't matter as much as the company's prospects. The opposite of a value investor.

Index funds. A portfolio of stocks or bonds that invests in all of the securities that make up a specific index, such as the Standard & Poor's 500 Index.

Individual Retirement Account (IRA). A way for individuals to put money away toward retirement. The income is not taxed until withdrawals begin after age 59 and one-half. In certain circumstances, the annual investment can be deducted from your income taxes as well.

Inflation. The rate of change in prices. The two primary indicators of inflation are the CPI and the PPI, which track the prices paid by consumers and producers. The rate can be calculated monthly, annually, or over the long term.

Initial public offering (IPO). The first time a company sells shares of itself to the public. The money that is raised goes to the company.

Institutional investors. Large companies who manage stock or bond portfolios such as banks, money managers, and mutual fund companies who buy and sell securities in large volumes.

Interest. The cost of money. If you loan money, you get interest. If you borrow money, you pay it. Simple interest is when you are paid interest only on the amount of the loan principal. Compound interest is interest earned on the principal plus any interest earned previously. Compound interest is better.

Investor. A person who puts money into growth assets over the long term.

Junk bond. A bond issued by a relatively unknown company or one that is in weak financial condition. The bonds pay a higher rate of interest because the investor runs a greater risk of default.

Large cap. A company with capitalization greater than $5 billion. Generally a lower risk stock investment.

Leading economic indicators. Components of a report released monthly by the U.S. Commerce Department's Bureau of Economic Analysis. It measures 14 items used to forecast the ups and downs in the total U.S. economy.

Leveraging. When you invest with borrowed money, such as with a margin account. Real estate investments are usually leveraged.

Limit order. When you make arrangements with a broker to buy or sell a security for you if it reaches a certain price.

Liquidity. The ability to easily convert an investment into cash without having a noticeable loss in value. Stocks and bonds are very liquid. Real estate is not.

Load. The commission or sales charge that is charged by mutual fund companies. It can be a front-end load or a back-end load.

Managed account. When you hire someone to manage your portfolio. They usually charge you a flat fee, such as one percent of the market value.

Margin buying. When you buy a security with money you borrowed from the brokerage firm. You can typically borrow up to 50% of the value of your account. You pay the broker interest to borrow money to buy securities. If your portfolio drops below a certain price, you will get a "margin call" from your broker. If you are buying on margin, you are a sophisticated investor.

Margin call. A demand that you put more money into your brokerage account because the value of your portfolio has dropped. Your portfolio is held as collateral for your margin loan. Your securities are sold if you can't pay the money in a timely manner.

Market. The term used to refer to the entire securities market, either for the U.S. or the world.

Market value. The price you could sell something for at a specific moment in time. An item is worth what someone else is willing to pay for it.

Mid-cap. A company that has capitalization greater than $1 billion, but less than $5 billion; generally average to higher risk investment.

Money manager. A person or company who gives investment advice for a fee. The person or company must be a Registered Investment Advisor with the SEC. People who manage mutual funds are also called money managers or portfolio managers.

Money market fund. A fund that invests in very short-term government and corporate debt. The net asset value of a money market fund does not change. (It is generally $1 per share.) This is a very liquid investment.

Money market mutual fund. A mutual fund that invests in short-term debt. It is a good place to put your savings.

Municipal bond. A debt obligation of a local or state government. General obligation (GO) bonds are backed by the municipality offering the bond. Revenues generated by a project back revenue bonds. For example, if a city issues a bond to pay for a toll bridge, it would use the tolls collected to pay the interest on the bonds. Revenue bonds are riskier than municipal bonds.

Mutual fund. A company that raises money from shareholders and invests the money in securities. Each investor owns shares in the fund. The more investors, the bigger the fund. Mutual funds can invest in a broad range of securities. There is no such investment as a "mutual fund." *You need to know what kinds of securities the mutual fund invests in before you invest in one.*

NASDAQ (National Association of Securities Dealers Automated Quotations System). A computerized stock exchange. Many technology companies and smaller companies trade on NASDAQ.

National Association of Securities Dealers (NASD). Operating under the supervision of the SEC, the NASD regulates broker activities and trading on NASDAQ.

Net asset value (NAV). The market value of one share of a mutual fund. It is determined by subtracting the liabilities from the assets and then dividing by the number of shares outstanding.

New York Stock Exchange (NYSE). Founded in 1792, it is the largest stock exchange in the U.S. Most large companies trade on the NYSE.

Odd lot. When you buy shares not in round lots of 100 shares of any stock. For example, 105 shares is an odd lot.

Online Trading. Trading stocks over the Internet.

Opportunity cost. The cost of passing up one thing (investment) in favor of another.

Option. The right to buy or sell a security at a certain price within a certain time. The right to buy is referred to as a "call" and the right to sell is called a "put." Buyers of calls expect the stock price to rise and buyers of puts expect the stock price to fall. Options trade on many exchanges and are always for round lots of 100 shares. *This is a pretty risky investment!*

Over-the-counter (OTC). Stocks and bonds that are not listed on the major exchanges are traded over-the-counter. Smaller companies and low value companies trade OTC.

Par. The face value of a stock or bond. That is, the dollar amount printed on the stock or bond. Also called "par value."

Penny stock. Stocks issued by small, relatively unknown companies for less than $1 a share. They are lightly traded, which makes liquidity a problem, and they are prone to price manipulation. *Don't buy them.*

Preferred stock. A class of stock that pays a specified dividend determined at the date of issue. Preferred shareholders are paid their dividends before common stockholders are paid. If the company goes bankrupt, preferred shareholders are paid before common stock shareholders.

Price/earnings ratio (P/E). The price of the stock divided by either its latest annual earnings per share (a trailing P/E) or its predicted earnings (anticipated P/E). The P/E is an important indicator of how investors feel about the stock. The higher the P/E, the more bullish people feel about the stock.

Privately held company. A company that is entirely owned by individuals or corporations. The stock does not trade on any of the stock exchanges. Privately held companies do not have to disclose any financial information. Small or family-owned businesses are usually privately held. This is the opposite of a publicly held company.

Producer Price Index (PPI). The measure of change in prices at the wholesale level. The PPI is broken into components by commodity, industry sector, and stage of processing. The CPI measures the change in prices at the consumer level.

Profit. How much money your money made. The amount left over after taxes and expenses.

Prospectus. A document that describes a securities offering or the operations of a mutual fund. The prospectus gives all of the details about the investment, such as fees, investment parameters, financial data, and history of the fund. IPOs and mutual funds are also sold by prospectus, stocks are not.

Proxy. When shareholders can't make it to the annual meeting of the company, they can sign a proxy that authorizes someone else to vote their wishes in their place.

Publicly held corporation. A corporation that has shares available to the public for purchase. The SEC regulates publicly held companies.

Registered representative. The formal name for stockbroker. The broker needs to be licensed by the NASD.

Risk. The possibility of loss or not gaining value. In investing, the possibility that your investment returns won't exceed the rate of inflation over the length of time of the investment or that they won't exceed the rate of U.S. Treasury bills, which is the risk-free rate.

Roth IRA. A contribution to a Roth IRA is not tax deductible. But the distributions are taken out of the IRA tax-free. If you make over a certain amount of money annually, you do not qualify for a Roth.

Round lot. A hundred shares of stock, the preferred number for buying and selling and the most economical unit when commissions are calculated.

Secondary Market. Once a security has been sold at the IPO, it is bought and sold on the secondary market.

Securities. Publicly traded measures of equity or debt.

Securities and Exchange Commission (SEC). The federal agency that regulates the finance industry.

Short selling. A technique used to take advantage of an anticipated decline in the price of a stock or other security. You borrow the stock from your broker and immediately sell it. Then you have to buy the stock back again to pay back your broker, hopefully at a cheaper price.

Simple interest. Interest calculated only on the original amount of the investment as compared to compound interest.

Small cap. Company with capitalization of less than $1 billion. Generally a higher risk stock investment.

Specialist. A member of a stock exchange who makes sure that the stocks they are responsible for trade in an orderly way. There are no specialists on NASDAQ.

Spread. The difference between the bid and asked prices of a security. This is also called the "broker's markup."

Stop-loss order. Instructions to a broker to sell a particular stock if its price ever dips to a specified level.

Street name. Securities held in custodian accounts are held in the name of the brokerage firm, not yours, but they belong to you on the books of the company. Holding stocks in street name makes trading a lot easier.

Tax deferred. When you are able to put off paying taxes until a later date. The income on your IRA and retirement plans is tax deferred until you begin taking out the money after the age of 59½. A Roth IRA can be distributed tax free after certain conditions are met. This is even better.

Tax exempt. Something you own that you don't have to pay taxes on. For example, a municipal bond is a tax-exempt security because you don't have to pay federal taxes on the interest.

Technical analysis. A computerized approach to analyzing companies. The technical analyst tries to forecast price movements by examining and charting the patterns formed by past movement in prices, trading volume, the ratio of advancing to declining stocks, and other statistics.

10-k. A financial report that all publicly held companies must file with the SEC. It is more detailed than a company's annual report. You can see it online under www.sec.com. Click on EDGAR database.

Tender offer. An offer to shareholders to buy their shares of stock. Tender offers are a key element of a take-over or buy-out of a company and are usually made at higher than market price to entice you to sell.

Time horizon. The amount of time you have before you need to use your money. How long you can have your money invested.

Total return. The return on your investment which includes capital appreciation, dividends, and interest earned.

Treasury bills, notes, and bonds. These are obligations of the U.S. Government. The government borrows money to pay for its expenses by issuing "Treasuries." A bill has a maturity of less than one year or less; a note has a maturity from 1 to 10 years; a bond has a maturity from 10 to 30 years.

12(b)1 fees. An extra fee can be charged by mutual funds to cover the costs of promotion and marketing.

Value style. An investor who looks for stocks that are undervalued. These stocks have low P/Es. This is the same as contrarian investing and the opposite of growth style.

Yield. In general, the return earned by an investment. Often used when discussing bonds.

Current yield is the interest rate based on the actual current price of the bond, which may be higher or lower than the face amount.

Yield to maturity is the rate that takes into account the current yield and the difference between the purchase price and the face value, with the difference assumed to be paid in equal installments over the remaining life of the bond.

Yield curve. A graph showing the structure of interest rates by plotting yields of all bonds of the same quality with maturities ranging from short to long term.

BIBLIOGRAPHY

Bach, David. *Smart Women Finish Rich: Seven Steps to Achieving Financial Security and Funding Your Dreams.* New York. Broadway Books. 1999.

Barron's Business Guides. *Dictionary of Tax Terms.* New York: Barron's Business Guides. 1994.

Barron's Financial Guides. *Dictionary of Finance and Investment Terms.* New York: Barron's Financial Guides. 1998.

Bogle, John C. *Bogle on Mutual Funds.* New York: Irwin Publishing. 1994.

Chopra, Deepak. *The Seven Spiritual Laws of Success.* San Rafael, California. Amber-Allen Publishing. 1994.

Dominguez, Joe, and Vicki Robin. *Your Money or Your Life: Transforming Your Relationship with Money and Achieving Financial Independence.* New York: Viking. 1999.

Ellerbee, Linda. *And So It Goes: Adventures in Television.* New York: G.P. Putnam's Sons. 1986.

———. *Move On: Adventures in the Real World.* New York: Putnam. 1991.

Friedman, Thomas L. *The Lexus and the Olive Tree.* New York: Anchor Books (division of Random House Inc.). 1999.

Heilbroner, Robert, and Lester Thurow. *Economics Explained; Everything You Need to Know About How the Economy Works and Where It's Going.* New York: Touchstone Books (division of Simon & Schuster). 1998.

Kiyosake, Robert T., and Sharon L. Lechter. *Rich Dad, Poor Dad, What the Rich Teach Their Kids About Money That the Poor and Middle Class Do Not.* New York: Warner Books. 2000.

Leeds, Dorothy. *Smart Questions to Ask Your Insurance Agent.* New York: Harper Paperbacks. 1992.

_____. *Smart Questions to Ask Your Stockbroker.* New York: Harper Paperbacks. 1993.

Leonard, Frances. *Money and the Mature Woman.* New York: Addison-Wesley. 1993.

Lordahl, Joann. *Money Meditations for Women.* Berkeley, Calif.: Celestial Arts. 1994.

Lynch, Peter, and John Rothchild (contributor). *Beating the Street.* New York: Fireside (division of Simon & Schuster). 1994.

_____. *One Up on Wall Street; How to Use What You Already Know to Make Money in the Market.* New York: Simon & Schuster. 2000.

Miller, Theodore J. *Invest Your Way to Wealth.* Kiplinger's Books: Washington, DC. 1994.

Morris, Kenneth M., and Alan M. Siegel. *The Wall Street Guide to Understanding Personal Finance.* New York: Lightbulb Press. 1997.

Morris, Kenneth M., Virginia B. Morris, and Alan M. Siegel. *The Wall Street Guide To Understanding Money & Investing.* New York: Fireside (division of Simon & Schuster). 1999.

O'Hara, Thomas E., and Kenneth S. Janke, Sr. *Starting and Running a Profitable Investment Club: The Official Guide from the National Association of Investment Clubs.* New York: Times Business (division of Random House). 1996.

Orman, Suze. *9 Steps to Financial Freedom.* New York: Random House. 1997.

Ponder, Catherine. *Dare to Prosper.* Marina del Rey, California.: DeVorss. 1983.

_____. *The Dynamic Laws of Prosperity.* Marina del Rey, California.: DeVorss. 1985.

_____. *The Prosperity Secrets of the Ages.* Marina del Rey, California.: DeVorss. 1986.

Roman, Sanaya, and Duane Packer. *Creating Money.* H. J. Kramer, Inc.: Tiburon, California. 2000.

Sheridan, Karen. *A Woman's Path to Abundance: A Seasonal Workbook for Growing Money.* Lake Oswego, Oregon: The Money Mystique. 1998.

_____. *Finding Your Way Out: A Common Sense Approach to Managing Debt*. Lake Oswego, Oregon: The Money Mystique. 1999.

_____. *Never Take NO for an Answer: One Woman, One Life, and the Money Mystique*. Wilsonville, Oregon: Bookpartners. 1997.

_____. *Your Money's Worth: A Common Sense Approach to Managing Your Money*. Lake Oswego, Oregon: The Money Mystique. 1999.

Stanley, Thomas J., and William D. Danko. *The Millionaire Next Door*. Atlanta, Georgia: Longstreet Press. 1996.

Tyson, Eric. *Investing for Dummies*. Foster City, California: IDG Books Worldwide. 1999.

Tyson, Eric. Mark Butler (Ed.). *Personal Finance for Dummies*. Foster City, California: IDG Books Worldwide. 2000.

White, Shelby. *What Every Woman Should Know About Her Husband's Money*. New York: Turtle Bay Books (division of Random House). 1992.

Zukav, Gary. *The Seat of the Soul*. New York: Fireside (division of Simon & Schuster). 1990.

REFERENCES

American Association of Retired Persons (AARP). 1999. *Profile of Older Americans*. The Program Resources Dept. Administration on Aging. U. S. Dept. of Health and Human Services.

Bureau of Labor Statistics. 1999. Abstract USDL 99-252. *Report on the American Workforce*. http://stats.bls.gov/opwork 99.

Carnegie Task Force on Meeting the Needs of Young Children. 1994. *Starting Points: Meeting the Needs of Our Youngest Children: The Report of the Carnegie Task Force on Meeting the Needs of Young Children*. New York: Carnegie Corporation.

Friedan, Betty. 1963. *The Feminine Mystique*. New York: W. W. Norton.

Gawain, Shakti. 1983. *Creative Visualization*. New York: Bantam New Age Books.

Medved, Diane. 1989. *The Case Against Divorce*. New York: Donald I. Fine.

Siegel, Jeremy, J. 1994. *Stocks for the Long Run*. Chicago: Richard D. Irwin.

Stanny, Barbara. 1997. *Prince Charming Isn't Coming: How Women Get Smart About Money*. New York: Penguin.

U.S. Census Bureau. 1999a. *Women in the United States: A Profile*. http://www.census.gov.Press-Release/www/2000/cb00-47.html

U.S. Census Bureau. 1999b. *Poverty: 1998 Highlights*. Supplement to the Current Population Survey.

U.S. Congress. 1992. House. Select Committee on Aging. Subcommittee on Retirement, Income, and Employment Report. *How Well Do Women Fare Under the Nation's Retirement Policies?* 102nd Congress. 2nd Session.

U.S. Department of Commerce. 1998. *News Release.* U.S. Census Bureau. Economics and Statistics Administration. 7.27.98. http://pr.aoa.dhhs.gov/aoa/stats/profile

U.S. Department of Commerce. 2000. News Report. *Profile of Nation's Women Released by Census Bureau.* U.S. Census Bureau. Economics and Statistics Administration. March 16. http://www.census.gov/Press-Release/www/2000/cb00-47.html.

U.S. Department of Labor. 1992. *Work and Elder Care Fact Sheet.* No. 5.98.

Williamson, Marianne. 1992. *A Return to Love.* New York: HarperCollins.

Zill, Nicholas, and Christine Winquist-Nord. 1994. *Running in Place: How America's Families Are Faring in a Changing Economy and an Individualistic Society.* Washington, DC: Child Trends. 15–17.

Karen Sheridan is a consultant and president of Money Mystique Asset Management Co., a Registered Investment Advisor.

She has more than twenty years' experience in business and finance on Wall Street and in Portland, Oregon. While on Wall Street, Karen was a vice president of Alliance Capital Management and The Bank of New York. In Oregon, she was vice president of PayLess Drug Stores and Capital Trust Company (US Trust). She is a frequent guest on radio and television talk shows and conference coach for Everywoman's Money Conferences.

Karen's meteoric rise from suburban housewife to Wall Street executive is chronicled in her first book, *Never Take NO For An Answer: One Woman, One Life and The Money Mystique*. She has published three workbooks, *Your Money's Worth: A Common Sense Approach to Managing Your Money; A Woman's Path to Abundance: A Seasonal Workbook for Growing Money*; and *Finding Your Way Out: A Common Sense Approach to Managing Debt*.

MORE NEW HARBINGER TITLES

DANCING NAKED
A psychologist who specializes in career counseling helps you embrace the uncertainties of today's job market and move beyond the issues that keep you from the work you love.
ITEM DNCE $14.95

TOXIC COWORKERS
Helps you recognize the personality traits that underlie inappropriate work behavior and teaches you how to develop effective strategies for dealing with them.
ITEM TOXC $13.95

UNDER HER WING
In-depth interviews with dozens of women provide a wealth of information that can be easily applied to any developing mentor relationship.
ITEM WING $13.95

FACING 30
A diverse group of women who are either teetering on the brink or have made it past the big day offer solace and support. *Rolling Stone* called what they had to say "funny, refreshingly direct, and tremendously helpful."
ITEM F30 $12.95

WOMEN'S SEXUALITIES
A well-known sex educator and therapist uses stories and results derived from her breakthrough sexuality survey to show readers how to accept and enhance their sexuality.
ITEM WOSE $15.95

MAKING THE BIG MOVE
Innovative exercises and practical suggestions help you transform relocation into a creative opportunity for personal growth.
ITEM MOVE $13.95

Call toll-free 1-800-748-6273 to order. Have your Visa or Mastercard number ready. Or send a check for the titles you want to New Harbinger Publications, 5674 Shattuck Avenue, Oakland, CA 94609. Include $3.80 for the first book and 75¢ for each additional book to cover shipping and handling. (California residents please include appropriate sales tax.) Allow four to six weeks for delivery.

PRICES SUBJECT TO CHANGE WITHOUT NOTICE.

Some Other New Harbinger Self-Help Titles

Family Guide to Emotional Wellness, $24.95
Undefended Love, $13.95
The Great Big Book of Hope, $15.95
Don't Leave it to Chance, $13.95
Emotional Claustrophobia, $12.95
The Relaxation & Stress Reduction Workbook, Fifth Edition, $19.95
The Loneliness Workbook, $14.95
Thriving with Your Autoimmune Disorder, $16.95
Illness and the Art of Creative Self-Expression, $13.95
The Interstitial Cystitis Survival Guide, $14.95
Outbreak Alert, $15.95
Don't Let Your Mind Stunt Your Growth, $10.95
Energy Tapping, $14.95
Under Her Wing, $13.95
Self-Esteem, Third Edition, $15.95
Women's Sexualitites, $15.95
Knee Pain, $14.95
Helping Your Anxious Child, $12.95
Breaking the Bonds of Irritable Bowel Syndrome, $14.95
Multiple Chemical Sensitivity: A Survival Guide, $16.95
Dancing Naked, $14.95
Why Are We Still Fighting, $15.95
From Sabotage to Success, $14.95
Parkinson's Disease and the Art of Moving, $15.95
A Survivor's Guide to Breast Cancer, $13.95
Men, Women, and Prostate Cancer, $15.95
Make Every Session Count: Getting the Most Out of Your Brief Therapy, $10.95
Virtual Addiction, $12.95
After the Breakup, $13.95
Why Can't I Be the Parent I Want to Be?, $12.95
The Secret Message of Shame, $13.95
The OCD Workbook, $18.95
Tapping Your Inner Strength, $13.95
Binge No More, $14.95
When to Forgive, $12.95
Practical Dreaming, $12.95
Healthy Baby, Toxic World, $15.95
Making Hope Happen, $14.95
I'll Take Care of You, $12.95
Survivor Guilt, $14.95
Children Changed by Trauma, $13.95
Understanding Your Child's Sexual Behavior, $12.95
The Self-Esteem Companion, $10.95
The Gay and Lesbian Self-Esteem Book, $13.95
Making the Big Move, $13.95
How to Survive and Thrive in an Empty Nest, $13.95
Living Well with a Hidden Disability, $15.95
Overcoming Repetitive Motion Injuries the Rossiter Way, $15.95
What to Tell the Kids About Your Divorce, $13.95
The Divorce Book, Second Edition, $15.95
Claiming Your Creative Self: True Stories from the Everyday Lives of Women, $15.95
Taking Control of TMJ, $13.95
Winning Against Relapse: A Workbook of Action Plans for Recurring Health and Emotional Problems, $14.95
Facing 30: Women Talk About Constructing a Real Life and Other Scary Rites of Passage, $12.95
The Worry Control Workbook, $15.95
Wanting What You Have: A Self-Discovery Workbook, $18.95
When Perfect Isn't Good Enough: Strategies for Coping with Perfectionism, $13.95
Earning Your Own Respect: A Handbook of Personal Responsibility, $12.95
High on Stress: A Woman's Guide to Optimizing the Stress in Her Life, $13.95
Infidelity: A Survival Guide, $13.95
Stop Walking on Eggshells, $14.95
Consumer's Guide to Psychiatric Drugs, $16.95
The Fibromyalgia Advocate: Getting the Support You Need to Cope with Fibromyalgia and Myofascial Pain, $18.95
Working Anger: Preventing and Resolving Conflict on the Job, $12.95
Healthy Living with Diabetes, $13.95
Better Boundries: Owning and Treasuring Your Life, $13.95
Goodbye Good Girl, $12.95
Fibromyalgia & Chronic Myofascial Pain Syndrome, $19.95
The Depression Workbook: Living With Depression and Manic Depression, $17.95

Call **toll free, 1-800-748-6273,** or log on to our online bookstore at **www.newharbinger.com** to order. Have your Visa or Mastercard number ready. Or send a check for the titles you want to New Harbinger Publications, Inc., 5674 Shattuck Ave., Oakland, CA 94609. Include $3.80 for the first book and 75¢ for each additional book, to cover shipping and handling. (California residents please include appropriate sales tax.) Allow two to five weeks for delivery.

Prices subject to change without notice.